Become A King

The mindset needed to take you to from

failure to success in life

Charles Sledge

Copyright © 2017 Charles Sledge

All rights reserved.

I am not a doctor. My books do not contain medical advice. All contents of my books are for informational, educational, and for entertainment purposes only. Reliance on any information of charlessledge.com & any books written by Charles Sledge is solely at your own risk. No liability will be assumed for the use of any information provided or contributed in my books. Consult a professional before following any of my advice.

Table of Contents

Table of Contents

Introduction

1 – Irrational Self-Confidence

2 – Growth Mindset

3 – Recruiting the Subconscious

4 – Ignoring Others

5 – Never Accept Average

6 – Be A Risk Taker

7 – Good Vs. Great

8 – Success Begets Success

9 – Failure

10 – Be A Trigger Puller

11 – Go Against the Grain

12 – Take Charge

13 – As You Think So Shall You Become

14 – Eternal Growth

15 – Beliefs Govern Behavior

16 – Have Hustle

17 – Never Compromise

18 – Be Positive

19 – Chart Your Own Path

20 – Self-Education

21 – Limiting Beliefs

22 – Action Creates Momentum

23 – Importance of Solitude

24 – Choose Your Life Or Have It Chosen For You

25 – Sanity Is Assumed

26 – Life Is A Choice

27 – Guilt

28 – The Purpose of Kingship

29 – 10 Steps to Begin Your Ascent

30 – 21 Attributes of A King

About the Author

Introduction

This book is written a bit differently from your average book. Instead of writing chapters and then filling in I choose to do a bit disjointed but more thorough approach.

I want you to absorb everything that there is to know on the subject of becoming a king. Absorbing the right mindset is something that takes time. But it is essential for your development as a man.

This is not something that can be rushed or something were you can refer to chapter four section A for the knowledge of what to do.

There are many subjects that are like that, this is not one of them. Many of the essays contained within work off one another, this is done on purpose.

You hear something once you may remember it. When you hear the same concept said in different ways or looked at from different angles you end up with a much more accurate and complete picture.

Think of it like this. Remember the tale of the men who all grasped a part of an elephant. One grasped the tail, the other the tusk, and another the leg. They all ended up with an incomplete idea of what an elephant is. One essay may address a certain part of a subject while another addresses the same subject in a different way.

Again this is done so that you the reader end up with a complete understanding of the subject at hand and are not left with incomplete knowledge. I don't intend to whet your appetite and then leave you high and dry. I intend to give you a full meal.

You will most likely want to reread this book a number of times so that the lessons contained within will sink deeper into your subconscious. To the point that they will become automatic. So you can embody all of the principles discussed within without having to think about them.

They will come naturally then. They will be a part of who you are. You will not have to think about them or about how to apply them. They will be you, they will be a natural part of you.

We all have a desire for greatness. It is a natural and healthy part of being human. Yet very few of us actually achieve anything resembling greatness.

This comes from not having the right mindset. I know there are many factors at play. Education, society, upbringing, and many others. However I know this, that with the right mindset you can achieve greatness. You can become the king you were born to be.

We may start at different places in life. I know there are people who started below me and people who started above me. However other people are irrelevant. What matters is what I do. What matters to you is what you do. What you choose to do with the cards you were dealt. With the life you were given.

Whining about the unfairness of it isn't going to do anything for you. Except keep you stuck, keep you in mediocrity. Keep you from moving forward and fighting back. From achieving your dreams.

So without further ado. It's time for you to man up and take charge of your destiny. To go out and conquer your fears so that your dreams will become reality. It's time to become a king!

1 – Irrational Self-Confidence

Nothing is more key to your success than an irrational belief in yourself. You must believe in yourself so much to the point that anyone doubting you would make you question their sanity.

Confidence

Confidence is something that means a lot of things to a lot of people. But everyone can agree on this confidence is key to life. To success with dating, making money, and achieving your goals. It doesn't matter what you are doing confidence plays an essential role.

Having faith in yourself. Something that is easier said than done. When you look into the mirror and look yourself in the eyes what feelings are stirred up?

Pride? Anger? Hatred?

If it's anything but the first than something needs to change. There can no room for self-doubt in your life. Seriously. Throw out all that negative programming that has been ingrained in you since the day you were born. You know what I'm talking about the "be careful", "you'll fail", and "that won't work".

You have to actively fight back against the negative programming.

The negative programming won't go away on its own. It must be actively fought. By reading books on having a positive mindset (such as this one), affirmations, and accepting yourself and who you are. The negative programming will begin to fall away and be replaced by your own positive programming.

You were created the way you were for a reason. A reason that you may not even know what it is (yet) but a reason nonetheless. Don't let others who aren't living up to their potential keep you from living up to yours.

That's why others say "you can't" and "it won't work" because they have given up on themselves and their lives. You succeeding would make them feel even worse than they currently do. Because of that they will fight against anyone who tries to rise above the crowd.

Belief in Self

What does it mean to believe in yourself?

It means that you value your own thoughts and actions. That when you make a decision and take action. You trust yourself. It doesn't mean you've never failed or that you try to achieve perfection. As that will never happen and always keep you unsatisfied. It means that you accept your imperfection yet realize at the same time your actions can be trusted.

You know yourself better than others do. You know what is best for you more than others know what is best for you. When you were a child it was wise to listen to the console and advice of others. Now doing the same is a liability. It would shut down your advancement faster than anything else. You must learn to listen to yourself and realize that what you say has worth, has lots of worth. That what you believe is something worth believing in.

Take the action that you think is right. Pull the trigger and deal with the consequences, whether they are positive or negative. The point is you made the decision and then you stuck with it. You didn't let others break you or sway you.

Get Rid of Doubt

Like stated before doubt has no place in your life. Doubt is the killer of faith. Doubt will keep you from moving. It will keep you tied down and a slave.

Doubt is not something that can be negotiated with. Not something that you can take half measured against. Doubt is insidious. It is a sickness, a cancer that will tear you up. Doubt is different from fear, it is okay to feel fear. Feeling fear is something that is inevitable. We all feel fear at one point or another.

Doubt is different. Doubt is that nagging voice (usually put there by others but then adapted as your own) that says "it won't work". Tells you that you cannot trust yourself. That you cannot trust your own judgement. That only others know what is best for you.

Nothing could be further from the truth. For better or for worse you must make the decisions in your life. You can talk with others especially those with wisdom but ultimately you and you alone decide where you are going to go. You are the pilot. You can take on a good co-pilot and crew but ultimately it is on you.

You Have Control

This is a good thing. The reason it is a good thing is because it means that you have control. When you realize that you have control you know that you direct where you go. Fate can push against you but it cannot stop you. The only person who can stop you is yourself.

Most people spend their whole lives stopping themselves. Either because they've been told they're not good enough for success, that success isn't possible so they shouldn't try, or they should just listen to others, to the crowd because otherwise they'd go in a wrong direction.

When you disregard the thoughts and opinions of others it frees you to rely on your own thoughts and opinions. When you begin to rely on your own thoughts and opinions you control your mindset. So you can decide you will believe in yourself.

You decide that the thoughts and opinions of others do not matter to you. That what truly matters is what you think of yourself. With that you can begin to cultivate positive thoughts and feelings about yourself and who you are. Which will lead to have an unshakable belief in yourself.

In other words irrational self-confidence in yourself.

You might have realized anyone who believes in themselves in the slightest is bad mouthed and put down. Yet for those who truly have confidence in themselves this doesn't affect them. What is the opinion of the fly to the lion? What the average person calls irrational is in fact the most rational line of thought you can have.

When given the choice (as you are given) why would you choose to work against yourself instead of for yourself? Having self confidence in yourself, believing in yourself completely and wholly is the only way to get on the right track to become all that you were destined to be.

No other way of thinking has the capacity, the ability to get you there. There is only one way and that way is by having "irrational" self-confidence in yourself.

2 – Growth Mindset

    I'm sure at some point in your life, you've felt stuck. Felt like things were not improving. That your business, relationships, or progress in the gym were not going anywhere. That what you have done to get to the point you're at isn't working anymore.

    To put it simply we've all been stuck in a rut before. Look around you everyone has been stuck in a rut before. Everyone has had times when they felt like things were just not working out and that no matter what they did things would not change.

Some people stay stuck in their ruts until the day they die. You don't want to be one of those people. Those people who stay the same day in and day out. Who are stagnate and not going anywhere. You know the kind. Work a forty hour per week job come home and smoke weed and play video games. Then jack off before falling asleep. Maybe you've been that person before. That's fine we've all been in a similar situation before. The point is not to stay like that. To grow past it into bigger and brighter things.

Preventing Ruts

You've heard it said before that "an ounce of prevention is worth a pound of cure". This applies to many things in life. One of which is the care of your mind and the prevention of stagnation. You see your mind like your body must be fed. It needs nutrition. Unlike your body it needs more than just physical nutrition. It needs mental nutrition as well.

    Your mind needs stimulation to grow. Just like your body. The influx of new information is what keeps your mind from getting stuck in the same loops (or ruts as we called them). When you are constantly learning new things your mind stays flexible, adaptive, and grows stronger.

It keeps you out of ruts or when you get in them you at the very least are able to get out faster. It helps you to deal with problems that life inevitably throws your way. You are more creative and responsive to life around you. The constant movement prevents you from getting stuck.

There Is No Stop

The majority of people believe that we can stay still in life. That we can be changeless. This is not true. The human mind, body, and spirit is always going in a direction. It is either ascending and growing better and stronger. Or it is descending and becoming weaker. There is no standing still. We are in constant motion. Our body, mind, and spirit changes from moment to moment. Not necessarily drastically but it changes.

Because of this we must make sure that we are doing activities that constantly move it in the right direction. We must cultivate good habits so that we ascend instead of descend.

For example. Every day I make sure to do the following things. The only exception to this is on weekdays or on short vacations and even then I find myself sticking to the list. Every day I read at least a chapter in a non-fiction book. The book could be related to writing, business, fitness, nutrition, attraction, or a variety of other subjects. The book has the opportunity to impact my life. It gives me new knowledge that I was not aware of before I opened the book. Every day I work out. Not balls to the wall PR setting but do a physical activity of some type. It used to be barbell complexes now it is usually three days of weightlifting with two of other activities. Such as going for a run, swimming, or playing a sport of some kind. I also try to have some sort of quiet time every day. It can be reading a book or just meditating.

Each and every day I take actions to better my mind, body, and spirit. I make time for these because I know if they are ignored all the progress that I have made will atrophy. Spending five years in the gym and one year out will not do you any good. Each and everyday things change for better or for worse. It's your job to make sure that those things are changing for the better.

Potential

We have just about an unlimited potential as to what we can be and do. The human mind never reaches it full capacity. There is always room for growth and improvement.

Which is a good thing. This means that we can grow until the day we die. We will never know it all and we will never do it perfectly.

Having a growth mindset sets you up for success. Because you grow into higher and higher "levels" of life. Like leveling up in a video game. You get stronger, smarter, and wiser. Allowing you to take on challenges that you could not have before. Eventually you get to the point where things that were once a challenge for you, don't faze you at all.

Things that once would have sent you running away or paralyzed in fear you face with confidence.

You face with an unshakable belief in yourself. Because you have grown in response to the challenges that life has thrown at you. You grow in response to stimulation. Like lifting a weight. At first maybe even the bar seemed heavy. Now you don't even notice it.

    The same can be done with life. All facets of it. However like in the gym it takes hard work. Not just hard work but hard and consistent work. This is a commitment. A commitment to yourself, a commitment to growth, a commitment to getting the most out of your life. A commitment to achieving your dreams.

Those who do not grow end up going extinct. It is the way of the world. It holds true in business, in relationships, and in your health. You have a choice to fall down to the ranks of mediocrity or to rise up to the status of a king. Like said before the choice is yours. Embrace your destiny and grow to the point where your dreams are reality.

3 – Recruiting the Subconscious

Your subconscious is one of the greatest assets that you have. Your subconscious controls the majority of your actions whether you are aware of it or not. What you put into to your subconscious seeps out through your thoughts and actions.

You subconscious can be one of your greatest enemies or your greatest ally depending on what you do with it. Depending on you. It can be used to propel you forward and upwards or it can be a weight around your neck dragging you to the bottom.

The key is you have to take control, you have to take responsibility for your subconscious. You must program it so that it is on your side. You must replace society's programming and replace it with your own. Just like you did in the last chapter.

Most of what you think, do, and feel does not come from you conscious mind but from your subconscious. Your conscious mind can only process so much at once leaving the vast majority of functions to the subconscious. For example if we had to constantly remember to breath, beat our hearts, and digest humans would have never made it as a species.

Your conscious mind works as a gatekeeper to your subconscious mind. Unfortunately most people's conscious mind is a crappy gatekeeper. It lets whatever comes to the door in. When this happens there is really not much of a point in even having a conscious mind. What's the point of a gate if it doesn't keep people out?

You must train your conscious mind to discriminate between what is good and worthy and what is not. Let's use two examples porn and the news. Both are negative influences in their own right. One corrupts your sexuality the other your outlook and understanding of the world. Both are poisonous to full development.

One is a cheap unhealthy substitute for sexuality and the other a cheap unhealthy substitute for knowledge. Like the difference between cooking a fresh kill and ordering mystery meat "chicken" nuggets One is true meat the other a cheap knockoff that is unhealthy for you.

Fill your subconscious with good things. Dwell on and think about good things. This doesn't mean block out reality as many would interpret it. Good news is not necessarily a good thing. Good news could make you lazy or complacent. Often good things are painful and hard. Working out is good. Reading is good. I'm not talking about good as in feels good, I am talking about good as in is actually good for you. Changes the meaning a bit doesn't it?

Scripts

We all have scripts or tracks in our mind that were placed there in our childhood. These scripts play themselves out in our day to day lives. These scripts are not permanent they can be modified and changed. By you inputting the good things we've been talking about.

For example. Quit saying "I can't" and quit making excuses. Here's the thing about excuses even when they are valid they do nothing to get you out of your situation. Meaning you could have a perfectly valid excuse but it's not going to do a damn thing to remedy whatever problem you're having. For example let's say your car broke down which made you late for work and your boss fired you. Now maybe you took care of your car and had it checked up often yet it happened to quit working that day. You still could have prevented it by having another form of transportation but that's not the point here. The end result is that you still ended up without a job.

So you say "It wasn't my fault my car broke down". So what? Does that change anything? No, it doesn't. You have to take responsibility for everything that happens to you. Don't blame others or blame fate. That will never get you anywhere. When you start taking responsibility you will start teaching your subconscious that you act against problems and struggles instead of letting them act on you.

Other negative scripts that you have acquired may be that you aren't worth much. Maybe your parents saw you as more of a problem than anything else. Maybe they had low self-esteem and took that out of you.

Being young and innocent you took these things to heart because you had no other way of interpreting it. Now as an adult you have the capacity to remove these negative messages and replace them with positive ones. No matter how deeply embedded they may be.

    Your brain can change, it is changing every moment of every day. New connections are being made. No matter your age, weight, or any other factor you brain can grow and improve. You are never stuck. Let me repeat that. You are never stuck, ever. Don't listen to anyone who will tell you otherwise. They are either liars or ignorant.

Two types of people that should be ignored.

Again fill your mind up with good things. Practice positive self-talk. Catch yourself whenever you put yourself down. Whenever you feel you are not worthy of something. Kill that thought. Become an effective gatekeeper for your thoughts and what you let in.

Another thing about the subconscious mind is that it doesn't discriminate. It doesn't reason or judge. It simply accepts. Whatever you let in, it will accept as truth, as good. Like a master telling an apprentice. The apprentice will accept whatever the master is saying. If the master gives the apprentice faulty information the apprentice will go and use it.

    Be careful what you put into your subconscious. As it runs the majority of your life. However once you get it working for you, you'll find that your success will accelerate at a level you've never seen before. It will take some work at first. After all you are replacing a lifetime of beliefs most of which are not helpful. But it is well worth it. Getting your subconscious mind on your own side is one of the greatest investments you can make and will change your life for the better.

4 – Ignoring Others

There is a time to listen and there is a time to forge on. There is a time to take the advice of others and times to ignore them. At some point in your life you must forge your own path. You must go in your own direction. You must go into uncharted territory.

This is what is required of a man. And to be a king you must first be a man. You must limit greatly who you listen to. The world is full of idiots, cheaters, scammers, losers, and whiners. Like I stated in The Primer humanity is like a bucket of crabs. When one gets close to making it out of the bucket the others all drag him back down ensuring that no one makes it out.

    Now don't get the idea that I'm telling you to disregard the wisdom of others, I'm not. What I am saying is that be selective with who you listen to. The vast majority of people should be ignored. Their advice, thoughts, and opinions. Taking in everyone's opinion or "hearing it from all angles" will keep you from ever taking off. It will keep you from ever making progress in life.

    My advice on this to look for people who have acquired what it is you're going after. Listen to people who have experience in what they are doing. You wouldn't take driving advice from someone whose never driven so don't take financial advice from someone who works a forty hour per week job and thinks saving ten percent of his paycheck will get him out of it. And even then you still have to make your own decisions.

 I've disagreed with people who know a hell of a lot more than me. Yet in the end things turned out alright. Because I choose to listen to myself. To what I know deep down is the truth. I follow my own compass. Sure I listen to the wise and those who are worth listening too yet in the end I make my own decisions.

I cannot tell you how much of a difference this has made in my life. To be my own man and make my own decisions. At first it was hard. It's human nature to try to fit in with the tribe, to not stand out too much because doing so may make you a target for exclusion from the tribe, which usually meant death. Yet even then the tribal leader was one who usually had the balls to stand out and take the lead.

   It's a damn good feeling to make your own way and stand on your own two feet. But it's not something that comes easy. The reward is great but the process is hard. That's the cycle of life for the most part.

By now you're noticing that that mindset is something that is trained. Something that requires concentrated effort on your part. Something that can only be done by you and you alone. Not outsourced to others.

The Trap of Average

To be great you can't accept being average. To be king you can't accept anything less. You should see average as just another stepping stone on your path to greatness. You should see being good at the things you focus on as just a stepping stone.

Complacency is dangerous, it's deadly. So many people think they've done "enough". They've worked enough, made enough, learned enough, and now they can sit back and coast on what they have accomplished. While there is value in taking a breath and looking at what you have done, if done for too long it is detrimental.

<u>Growth only stops at death.</u>

And even then maybe not, who knows what comes after that. The point is you never know when enough is truly enough. Look at all the people who lost their jobs during the recession. Look at people who thinking they have enough saved for retirement suddenly have to have an emergency surgery and their account takes a huge hit. I'm using money as an example but it applies across all fields of life.

People always think they are prepared. The average person always thinks that they have enough. A lot of this type of thinking comes about because having more generally takes more work. Something the average person will avoid like the plague, to their detriment.

Then when hard times come the average person is screwed. Because they didn't prepare properly. They thought that listening to the news, media, what their teachers taught them, the "experts", friends, and family would be enough. Right?

After all that many people can't be wrong, can they? The majority is always right, aren't they? That's at least how the myth goes. Despite what the average Westerner believes the majority is actually not a good source of advice. As a matter of fact the only thing the majority is good for is.

One. Being taken advantage of by those at the top.

Two. Modeling what behaviors to do the opposite of.

The majority, the crowd, the "unwashed masses" are not who you should follow. The elite, the winners, the kings of this modern world are who you should listen to. The innovators, leaders, the brave. However this group makes up a very small percentage of people. Just because someone has wealth or fame does not make them part of this group either.

You must be selective with who you listen to and generous with who you ignore. This doesn't mean you need to be an ass to everyone. I love my family and friends. Yet they all know that most likely I'm not going to listen to them and I'm going to go my own way and do my own thing. They respect this. Others don't but that isn't my problem.

    Remember when we talked about being a good gatekeeper for your subconscious. A good part of this is not just selecting what too listen to but also ignoring the majority of messages and people. This is one of the reasons solitude is so great for learning and development. When you are left alone with your own thoughts it helps you to stay centered. To train your mind to become what it has the capacity to become.

    We truly have limitless potential. No human comes close to

reaching their fullness and they never will. You can be one hundred times greater than you are today. If you have the drive, the fight, and the right mindset.

5 – Never Accept Average

Average. Since childhood kids are often told that it's okay to just show up, to not worry about competing, that there is nothing wrong with being average.

Part of this I agree with. There is nothing necessarily "wrong" with being average. However the rest is wrong and the wrong mindset to instill in the young so that they may have a prosperous future.

This book isn't about being okay, this book is about being the best. To be the best you must accept nothing but the best.

    As an example let's say you are an athlete and wish to one day compete in the Olympics. One day at practice your coach talks to you about how well you're doing as you have blown away every other individual on the team. You thank the coach but then proceed to practice. Your eventually get to the point you're one of the best in your area. Your parents are proud, your school is proud, your friends are proud yet you stay at the grind.

    Some friends question why you don't go out with them and do things. After all you're "already good enough". Maybe even your parents and coach becomes worried too. They talk to you about "balance" and "there's nothing wrong with taking a break".

Despite all this you keep at it. And this is why, because you are not okay with being "good enough" you are not okay with fulfilling the expectations of others. You have your own goal and your own quest. Your own standards that you want to fulfill. Until you fulfill those standards you are going to keep at it.

Some people stop after making their first million. After all isn't that what the average person would do? They try to coast and soon find out that a million isn't a lot of money. Then they're back at it. Often to repeat the cycle time and time again.

Then you have the winner. The person who isn't okay with "doing alright" or "just enough". Both of these phrases are insults to him. His personal standards are high and he busts his ass so that he can meet them. After making a million he has his sights set on ten million and so on and so forth.

Most people won't understand him. That's because most people are by definition average. A lot of people don't understand that to rise to the top, to make tons of money or be the best at your field. You have to be unbalanced to a degree. Not in drugs and reckless spending but in work and the influx of knowledge.

To be the best you must have a drive, a hunger, an obsession. Where you work day and night at it until your dreams are hammered into reality by the work of your hand. Your mind and body are devoted to a single purpose and that single purpose fuels your every action.

You must be willing to go above and beyond what the "average" person would do to be king. Put in the hours, the effort, the thought. When you look at the best they are never wishy washy about their goals and desires. They have a precise laser like focus on where they are going and what it is that they want to accomplish. Anything that gets in their way is destroyed because their drive is so strong.

Where your thoughts are focused is where your future lies. Your thoughts create your actions and your actions create your destiny. There is a powerful unalterable link between your mind and your reality. What you think and what you get and ultimately where you go. Make sure your thoughts are putting you in the right direction.

The Extra Mile

Many powerful individual's success can be attributed to simple not giving up. To their willingness to keep going despite rejections, fear, and everything else. Their single minded focused allowed for complete dedication to their cause. Their faith in themselves, their goals, and their dreams allowed them to prosper where others failed. To find abundance where others found scarcity.

It's sad how many give up right before they are about to make it. They take a shot which is good but then after a year or so they hang it up because it didn't meet all of their desires right away. You see this in success stories as well. People who were just about ready to give in when something happened that changed the course of their life. Had they given in and been okay with being average they never would have gotten to the point that they are at now.

    Successful people, kings, have a distaste even a hatred for average. Not for the average person but for being average themselves. Don't hate someone for not living up to your standards that is their choice and hate is wasted energy that will only bring you down. Hold yourself to your standards don't worry about others, they are not your concern. Focus on yourself, on your own goals and actions. Your own success.

If you don't have something that fires you up. That motivates you day in and day out and that provides you will the will to keep going you are going to have a very hard time rising above the ranks of average. You need to find your mission and your goal in life.

The thing that will help you to rise above and take the lead. The thing that will be on your heart and mind day and night until it is accomplished. Figure this out and then harness it to propel you to greatness. Ignore the average and rise above them.

Do this and it will only be a matter of time before you are living the life that you want and achieving your dreams. It sounds simple and it is. But it is not easy. It will take time and it will take effort. Put in both and you will be well on your way to becoming a king.

6 – Be A Risk Taker

You're told your entire life to be careful. To take it easy. To pause before you make decisions. Take it slow. Essentially to protect the little that you have because we live in a world of scarcity.

Part of this I agree with. If you don't have the right mindset we do live in a world of scarcity. The world we live in is harsh and brutal. However there is more than enough money/women/success or whatever you desire to go around for those who have the balls to go after it.

There is an abundance of whatever it is you desire. Not only is there an abundance but you can have it. But you will not get it remaining where you are at. Einstein said that one definition of insanity is doing the same thing over and over again and expecting different results. Meaning that what got you to where you are will not get you to where it is that you want to go.

To get to where you want to go you have to take action. You have to get momentum going. The best way to do this is to be a risk taker. Someone who surges ahead, who takes chances, and who isn't afraid to fail. Those are the people who will achieve what they want, those are the people who others will wonder how did they do it.

    Hunkering down and holding on tightly to what little you have will only ensure that whatever little you have will eventually run out. You have to keep expanding and growing. Empires that stagnate die. You must keep forward momentum going. It's much easier to keep something in motion than it is to start something in motion.

    You probably remember the story of the tortoise and the hare. The slow steady tortoise and the fast lazy rabbit. The moral goes that slow and steady wins the race. I have to disagree slow and steady will get you killed in today's world. Don't get me wrong being fast and lazy won't get you much either. To be the best and thrive, to be the king, you have to be both fast and steady. You have to take action, take risks, and put your nuts on the chopping block and then do so continuously for extended periods of time.

Take risk after risk after risk. Until you have acquired success. Don't hesitate too long. It's better to fail in action than to wait in inaction. Fail forward in forward motion. If you're going to get hit at least get those extra couple of yards.

Fate

Fate is not the ultimate determinant of where we end up. Fate is an influencer but not the decision maker. You are the decision maker. You should never rely on luck as luck is something that lazy people use to describe people more successful than them. After all there is no way that it could be their own fault.

The Greek myths have stories of heroes who defied the Gods. Who stood up against them by their own will. Now I am no expert on the Greek myths and do not claim to be. But a man making his own path against the forces of chance or against fate itself has always been something that is idealized and looked up to.

You can be the master of your own fate as well. Through hard work, dedication to your cause, and through relentless action taking and taking risks until you achieve what it is you desire.

Say a man is born with average looks and a poor upbringing. He was bullied in school and was never taught to be a man by his father who left him and his family when he was young. In high school he took his best friend to the prom. Who ended up ditching him for some guy who bullied him.

Anyways this kid realizes that life isn't going to do him any favors. If he wants something he is going to have to better himself until he doesn't have to rely on fate to help him. He takes matters into his own hand. Time for college comes around. While there he forces himself to go out and interact with people, read good books, and go to gym all things he avoided or never did in the past.

He starts flirting with girls he finds attractive and asking them on dates. At first he gets blown out of the water at every turn but he figures that's fine, I'll just keep working. And he does so.

A year passes. Now this kid has some respectable muscle on him, he knows more than the majority of his peers, and has banged five chicks not exactly a record breaker but considering he was a virgin at the beginning of the year nothing to laugh at either.

This kid graduates and finds that others who he once considered better than him now come to him for advice. Girls he had crushes on in high school pretty much beg for him to screw them. He starts and runs a successful business. He knows it wasn't because of fate he got to where he was but because of his own sweat, blood, and tears.

Now let's compare him with another guy. This guy was born with good genetics, his was raised in a two parent home and his dad took an active interest in his son's development into manhood. He loses his virginity in the 9th grade to a girl two years older than him. He plays football and is pretty popular.

At prom he takes some nerd's he makes fun of best friend and bangs her brains out at a party later. Goes to college and pretty much repeats high school but on a grander scale. He graduates with a degree in business and works for his dad's company making a relatively good income.

Anyways two men, two different paths. One created his own fate the other got lucky. Now let's say fate takes a turn for both of them, for the worse. Who is going to cope with it better? Who is going to be able to rise up? Who is more used to taking risks and putting himself out there? One was raised with an umbrella over him while the other had the drainage pipe over his head. Who's going to weather the storm better?

Good fate can ultimately be a curse if it leads to complacency, laziness, or other bad qualities. Just like hard luck can the catalyst to propel you to be all that you can be.

How effective would the Marines have been during WWII if they had it easy during training? Bad fate often creates good men. Now say you've actually had a pretty decent life. No major crises, just regular living. This doesn't mean that you can't be great. Don't think you need some great tragedy or zero to hero story to become great.

People with bad fate still turn out losers all the time, they just generally get the understanding that life is either going to make or break them a lot earlier than the others. If you have the drive, fight, and desire regardless of your fate you can be great. And don't forget to take risks.

7 – Good Vs. Great

From bad too good to great that's how it works right? Sometimes it very well can work that way. However oftentimes good can become a trap. Once someone has enough to get by and be reasonable comfortable they often get off their path and get sidetracked.

Sometimes it's harder to go from good to great than from bad to great. I've said it before when you're at the bottom you lose a lot of fear, you don't have a problem taking chances, and you have that hunger that is so essential to success.

When things are going alright you have to make your own drive, you have to motivate yourself to get out of your comfort zone.

Think about it like this. You have me who didn't want to work in what I majored in. Bounced around trying different things thought about the Marines, the Sheriff Department, and a couple other things that didn't pan out for me for a number of different reasons. Eventually I found out that many people create the lives they want, that there is an another option aside from being the average American. So I devoured all that I possibly could on building your own business and creating your own life.

While most people I know go from day to day without growth without progress because they have a job they're reasonably comfortable with and have a life their reasonably comfortable with. By societies standards they are doing good, they are doing normal.

Meanwhile I bounced around. I did not want to do what my major was. I had debt. Overall I wasn't exactly in a good position. Yet I didn't fear because I knew that I could create what I wanted. I knew that I could create a life that I loved. A life that I didn't need the weekend to escape from. I never wanted to be one of the TGIF crowd. I didn't want to live around seventy percent of my life hating it. I didn't want Monday to Friday at five to suck and have two days to recuperate.

I was hungry. I didn't have a comfy job. I had to move back in with my parents. Meanwhile others in my age group had homes, some were getting married, and jobs they enjoyed. Meanwhile I was going in a completely different direction.

Because I was not satisfied with my life. I wanted more, I always wanted more it just took me awhile to realize it. I wasn't going to do the forty hour per week, get married, and get a home like so many people do. That path may be right for some people but I knew deep down in my heart that it wasn't right for me. I was hungry for greatness. No, I was starving for greatness.

Every day working on my blog, reading books, writing books like the one you're reading now, improving myself, taking chances. I wanted success bad. I thought about success. I thought about making it. About having to never worry about money, about living a life of freedom and living my dreams, and about changing the lives of millions of people. Every day I am working towards my goals and every day I get closer to achieving all that I can in the time given to me and more.

If I had a steady job and a reasonably attractive girlfriend and a place to live. I may have never gone down this path. I would have been alright being good and never concerned myself with being great. Again ultimately it is up to you.

You may have a good job, nice house, and a wife or girlfriend you enjoy. You can still be great but you must discover you reason why.

It'll be different from me. You must find your own reasons for why you want greatness. Part of it could be for your family, friends, or society but ultimately it has to be for you and you alone. You must live your life for yourself otherwise the motivation will dry up fast and you'll be stuck at good.

    Here is an exercise that I would recommend that you do. Take out a sheet of paper and write down what it is you want out of life. Don't worry about being realistic at the moment simple write down your desires. Write down at least ten things. Then visualize achieving those things. Think about what it would be like to accomplish those things on your list and how your life would be changed.

    Rewrite this list every day for a month. Focus your mind on it. After rewriting it visualize the achievement of each thing on the list. Print out pictures if that helps but visualize. This should only take about fifteen minutes or so.

Do this for a month and be on the lookout for opportunities to make progress on these fronts. For ways to advance. The point of this is to get your mind focused. You have probably heard of "The Law of Attraction" which essentially states that what you think about you get.

While this has been taken in some unfortunate directions. Namely sit on your ass and think about something and poof it will magically be yours. But the original law had much truth to it. What your mind focuses on increases. At the end of the month write down all the advancements that were made towards the goal. Don't limit yourself in this. Don't expect any goal to take years, months, or whatever let it happen as it happens.

    Finding your reason why is one of the most important parts of becoming successful. Find your why will help propel you through the good period to the great. Finding your why will get you from bad to great and beyond. If you are currently at a good level of something you want to be great at, be careful to not get to lazy. Propel yourself forward if you ever get stuck remember to refer to your why and your ultimate goals. These will keep you strong and keep you going until the end.

8 – Success Begets Success

Humans are lazy by nature. Give them a choice between action and inaction while achieving similar results and they will side with inaction. After all it is only logical. Why waste energy, right? Because of this humans look for shortcuts in everything. One of the prime ways humans do this is through the forming of habits. Instead of having to do something consciously time and time again humans fall into patterns or habits. This saves both time and energy.

Because of this people get stuck in cycles. Cycles that can either work for them and propel them to greatness or can work against them and bring them down. When people are doing well they tend to keep doing well and when people are doing poorly they tend to continue doing poorly. You've probably heard "the rich get richer and the poor get poorer" before. This is just one example of this concept in action.

Another is that twenty percent of men sleep with eighty percent of women. You've probably hit a dry spell that seemed to last forever only to hit a week where you slept with more women then you did in the three months previous. The key is to stay in positive cycles. Success begets success.

This doesn't mean you should fear failure as failure is what paves the way to success. What this means in that the habits that will bring you success only get stronger the longer that you stay on the path. Cultivating habits of growth and learning will pay out exponentially the longer that you do it.

Let's use reading about business as an example. You start out reading about entrepreneurship and start a website. You spend three months working on it, improving it, and building it. After three months you are making some money off ads you have on the site. Enough to pay for going out on the weekends while also covering the cost of the blog itself.

You continue learning, growing, and improving. It's now been a year since you started. Your site is one of the top in its niche. You are now making enough money to quit your day job that you hated. You now devote all your time to learning how to improve your site, help others, and learning more about content in your niche or site's topic.

Three years have gone by. You now run a company that employs multiple people. You make more money than you know what to do with. Your goal now is to help others as much as possible to achieve their dreams and get out of a job they hate. Your site name is now known all across the world and is synonymous with your niche or site topic. The entire time you have devoted yourself to learning and growing.

At first it got you some beer money. Nice but not exactly life changing. Then after that you were able to quit your job. A dream come true for you. Others are jealous, not to mention a bit confused, that you were able to quit your job from running a website. Finally it was able to get you to a place you wouldn't have even dreamt about when you started. Because you took the time to learn, grow, and improve you were able to live the life of your dreams. Actually a life beyond your dreams as what you realized could be accomplished extended with each advancement in your mind and life.

But this all started in your mind. Your website wouldn't have improved and your brand spread if it didn't first happen in your mind. It was your dedication to improving yourself and getting "stuck" in that positive habit loop that brought you to the point where you were living beyond your wildest dreams.

Through the right thinking and right ideas you will create the right habits and when the right habits are created you will then get yourself in the right loop. When you get yourself in the right loop you will be successful. When you are successful it is easier to become more and more successful.

When you are a failure. Not failing but a failure. Meaning someone who doesn't try, who is stuck is a loop of negative habits. You must work to dig yourself out of the negative loop you are in. If not you will never be able to build up enough momentum to get going.

    This is usually the hardest part. Making the switch from bad habits to positive habits. Like starting a company compared to keeping it going. Like starting a fire compared to keeping it going. Forming energy or switching energy is the toughest part. Once things are going in the right direction it becomes a bit easier. Not effortless but easier. You are working for yourself instead of against yourself. Like stated before when you get your subconscious mind working for you instead of against you, it makes a huge difference. The same applies to your habits, which while separate from your subconscious mind they both have an tremendous effect on your development.

Look at it like this imagine you're kayaking on a river that runs from North to South. Three miles to the North of your current position is everything you've wanted, is exactly what you have been looking for.

Your habits are like the flow of the river. Negative habits would be like the river flowing to the South and positive habits would be like the river flowing to the North. It will be a lot easier to get to your destination with the river flowing in the direction you want go in. With the river flowing against you, you can still get to your destination but it's a hell of a lot harder. Whereas with the river working with you it becomes exponentially easier. You still have to steer the canoe, avoid rocks, be aware of what's going on but overall your journey will be a lot smoother.

The more you succeed the easier it becomes to succeed. Get into the correct cycle and then your effort can be focused on other areas of your life. Like creating a best-selling book that earns you money even while you sleep. At first it took a lot of worker learning about the subject or outlining the story. Then sitting down and writing it took effort and time as well. Yet in the end it now works for you to help you. Now when you go to write another book you will already have your name out there and people familiar with your work. Which will help you sell any other books that you end up writing. Early lots of effort with little reward but with time that switches and you get little effort with big reward. It's all about cultivating the right habits to get into the loop of success.

9 – Failure

Failure is something we are trained to avoid. Failure is something we try to experience as little of as possible in our lives. This is a mistake. Most of us have the concept that in one direction is failure and in the other direction is success. So every time we experience a failure we are moving further away from success and every time we experience a success we are moving further away from failure.

However this isn't how it works. Failure is not in the opposite direction of success but in the same direction. Imagine it like this say you're a knight who wants to get to a castle. This castle has lots of food, hot princesses, and everything else a knight could desire. But between him and that castle is a swamp. A swamp that cannot be avoided no matter which way he goes. The wrong idea would be to avoid the swamp or every time he experienced the swamp to turn back around. The reason being to get to the castle with the hot princesses and warm food you have to make it through the swamp.

The swamp is failure and the castle is success. Failure lies on the path to success not away from it. Failure is a perquisite for success. This doesn't mean you have to fail at a certain time and certainly don't try to fail but that failure will come. For example don't go out and start a business then when things get hard shut it down and declare "well failure is the path to success" or "well everyone fails at first". You are misinterpreting this truth. Failure will come without you having anything to do with it and it might not be catastrophic. It could just be inconveniences and uncomfortable circumstances you have to overcome to get where you want to go. Never try to fail but when you do realize you need to keep moving on.

The Difference Between Failing and Being A Failure

There is a big difference between someone who fails at something and someone who is a failure. Failing is generally a verb, an action. While being a failure is a noun. Failing is okay. It happens to everyone. Being a failure is not okay.

Failing means you attempted something and it didn't turn out the way you wanted. You didn't get what you want. Trying to deadlift 405 for your first time and losing your grip at the lockout is an example of failing. Asking a girl out but getting rejected would be an example of failing. Opening a business and failing to capitalize on your customers would be an example of failing. The point is failing is not bad. As a matter of fact it is good. It means you're trying it means you're going for it. When you fail you learn from it and get better.

    Contrast this with being a failure. A very big difference. When you are a failure it means the opposite of failing. When you are a failure you don't attempt new things, you don't try. You sit back and whine or blame or make excuses. When you're a failure you don't try to succeed, you don't take chances and go for it. You are lazy and relying on fate, circumstances, or others to get you out of whatever situation you are in. You never take responsibility for your situation as you are caught up in being a victim which will keep you a failure for all eternity if you let it.

For example. In the situations above where we gave examples of failing the failure would have never even gotten that far. He would have never attempted to reach a new max, never gone for a girl he found attractive, and never started his own business. As these things are things that require initiative. Require that you take the responsibility for how your life and the interaction is going to turn out.

The good news about all this is that it is easy to not be a failure. All you have to do is start taking action. Start going for it and failing. It doesn't matter if you're dead broke living in your mom's basement. If you're actively working to better yourself and change the situation that you are in you are not a failure.

Fail Your Way to Success

The road to success is paved with failure. Doesn't mean that you seek failure out. You should always go for success just understand failure will be part of the journey. Failure helps you learn, it helps you get over your fears, and it helps you to grow as a person. As a personal example before I ran my current blog I had another about a year before. I got an article on a large site and was steadily increasing traffic. However I ran into issues of supporting the blog as I was not making any money from it. Though I truly enjoyed writing and the feeling of helping others I had to shut it down. It sucked but I learned a hell of a lot from it.

    I learned how to better prepare for running a website. How to write posts and set up a clean looking site. How to start networking and how important it is to interact with your readers. So though I failed it wasn't a failure. It wasn't a failure because

I learned so much from it and because I kept going for my goal. I changed things around and did things differently this time allowing me to keep the site up and continue my work.

So when you start experiencing failure realize you are on the path to success. Realize that being a failure is different from failing and in many respects the two are opposites. Don't blame others or refuse the responsibility for your own life. It is all on you. Anything that you want to accomplish in this life is on you and you alone. So get out there are start failing so you never join the ranks of failures.

10 – Be A Trigger Puller

Thoughts alone aren't going to get you to where you want to go. They must be followed by action. When it comes down to it you must be a trigger puller someone who is able to make the hard decisions and doesn't back down when things get rough.

Look at it like this. Ultimately taking an action is the only thing that matters. Let's say you were given the idea for Apple ten years before Steve Jobs had an inkling of what he wanted to do. Let's say you talked to your friends about it and let's say they were supportive about it. Let's say you started researching ways for it to come about and had a bullet proof plan lain out. Yet you got caught up in other things and never took action. Now years later you look back and think "Hey I had that idea!" but it doesn't matter.

 This happens all the time to people. They have an idea that will take them to where they want to go but they never act on it. The story remains unwritten, the invention never happens, and the thought drifts away never to materialize into an action. The world belongs to the action takers. To the ones who have the guts to pull the trigger.

The expression trigger puller comes from someone who is willing to take the shot. A gun is worthless if you don't have the correct mindset to pull the trigger. A knife or even a heavy rock is more effective than a gun if the trigger is never pulled. You have to be willing to take action even if there might be consequences for that action.

The timid will never get far in life. Those who do not follow through will never get far in life. Going back to the example before we've all probably had flashes of insight where we thought "that would be a good idea". Yet without the follow through nothing will come of it. You could have the greatest idea in the world but without action it will remain just that, an idea. And ideas in and of themselves are not going to get you what you want. You must bring them forward into the world through action.

You must move things forward. In your business, in your relationships, and in your life. Every aspect of it. Think about it. Even when you are on a date with a woman you are the one who has to move things forward. You're the one who has to initiate the interaction, the kiss, and the sex. It's all on you.

Life is not going to get better for you if you don't have the balls to make decisions. It you don't pick a side and then stick with it. Doesn't mean you can't ever change but just pick a direction and then go in it. Stop waiting around for the right circumstances, for others to take the lead or to approve, and for the right signs. When you do this you're putting your life and the direction of your life in the hands of others. Other people and fate will never guide you where you want to go. And will often try to hurt you over help you.

Let me give you an example from my own life. When I started

writing my first book I knew nothing about writing, editing, or producing a book. I had no friends who knew anything about writing or mentors other than research I did on the internet. I figured I would figure things out as I went. I had always learned best by throwing myself in the middle of something and working from there, so that is what I did with the book.

At first I didn't worry about editing or it being polished. I simply wrote. I took action every day trying to hit my word count and giving value. I tried to pour everything I knew into the page and would worry about the rest when I got to it. After finishing the manuscript I again wasn't sure where to go for editing.

I looked at a number of different options but was flat broke and decided to edit the work myself. Again I knew nothing about editing so just dove into it. I recognized obvious things like misspelled or misplaced words and researched other editing tips along the way.

After that I began researching how to publish a book on Amazon and figured out I needed a cover. I went around and again found a bunch of expensive covers but none that were what I needed. I had a cover made off of Fiverr. A website that started off where people would offer services for five dollars, though they have expanded past that now.

I uploaded the manuscript and the cover image I had made to Amazon and my first book was published. It was a great feeling. To have my work available to others especially since a year before I could not even have fathomed having my own book out in the world, yet there it was.

My point here is that I never waited, I never hesitated. I could have waited for others and perhaps did a better job of writing or editing it. Or waited and found someone who could have made a better cover.

Or a hundred other things, but I didn't. I took action and made plenty of mistakes and wouldn't have it any other way.

Take action. Be reckless over cautious. Make a mistake over sitting still. Remember it's better to fail than to do nothing. I'm serious. I'd rather strike out than never swing. I mean sure I'd rather hit a home run but that will never happen unless I'm also willing to strike out.

The guy who drunkenly stumbles forward tripping over every rock will win a race before a guy who doesn't take any action. I'm not saying to be the drunken stumbling guy in life, simply that no matter where you're at or who you are. If you take action you can make it. If you move forward you can make it. If you can pull the trigger you can make it. So go out and take action.

11 – Go Against the Grain

"The objective of life is not to be on the side of the majority, but to escape finding oneself in the ranks of the insane" this was said by the Roman emperor Marcus Aurelius. In the Western world we have been brain washed to believe that the masses are intelligent beings. That the majority is in the right. That everyone has their "rights" and is divinely given them. I'm not here to dispute or agree with this but to outline something. The mass of people are general not much more than zombies or animals.

This isn't an insult as I wish for all people to transcend the cages around their mind but it is a fact. It is simply stated to illustrate a point. Normal or average is not good. Just because the majority does something does not mean you should do it.

The majority of people are not rich, the majority of people are not in good health, the majority of people do not have the sex lives they want, the majority of people gave up on their dreams a long time ago. Does this sound like a group you want to associate with or be a part of?

Remember hate isn't going to help you. It will only bring you down. Often people who are scared of their own inferiority will act superior to the "masses" yet this just highlights that they are just as much a part of them as any other. To be above the masses doesn't mean to look down on them. A truly rich man does not look down on the average man for being average. He doesn't feel hatred or distaste for him. If a man is truly rich he will want to help the average man rise up to where he is in life.

Stand Out

Many if not most people are scared to stand out from the crowd. They work their whole lives to blend in and not be noticed. They think the thoughts that most think, act the way most act, and believe the things that most believe. They do this often out of fear. Fear of ridicule, fear of alienation from the group, and fear dredged up by their own insecurities.

    They don't want to go against the grain because it causes friction. They have been taught from an early age that friction is bad. That people disagreeing with them means that they are doing something wrong. Most likely some if not all of this sounds familiar. You've probably been in the same situation before. It might have been years ago or maybe it was a couple of minutes ago.

This can be overcome through the application of the principles in the book. You must learn that friction is okay. That standing out from the crowd doesn't mean you are wrong or that you are insane. Remember humanity operates on a bell curve. Meaning that not being normal could mean you're doing that much better than others as opposed to worse. Most people see deviating from the norm as that means they are in the wrong. When it could be just as true that the majority is the one in the wrong. It takes a lot of guts to go against the will of the majority but it can be tremendously freeing. Not to mention the more you do it the easier it becomes.

You've probably heard the stories of some of the most successful people of our time. That Edison's teachers said he was an idiot or that Carnegie was born dirt poor and many others. These men all were not in the majority. There was something different about them. I'm sure they all had insecurities at times when they took steps to stand out and go against the grain but they stuck with it. And because they stuck with it they were able to reap the rewards of ascending above the majority.

When they did this they were then able to pave the way for many more to come after them. Look at Henry Ford by not being part of the majority he was able to enrich the majority in countless ways. There is probably no one you know who doesn't use a car for transportation.

Don't worry about the opinion of the majority. The majority of people believe in things that greatly limit them in life and they think everyone should think this way. They use shame and fear to get people to fall in line. Yet when someone doesn't fall in line they are ridiculed yet they go far beyond any who ridicule them.

If you don't have haters you're probably doing it wrong. Having haters, people who doubt you is a good sign. Getting polarized reactions from people is a good thing. You have to turn some off to turn others on. If you don't stand for anything you won't ruffle any feathers but you won't live life either.

Don't let the majority castrate your mind or your balls. Don't be afraid to take a stand, break away from the pack, and chart your own course. Average sucks. It really does. You never want to end up in the ranks of the zombified majority.

You want to be a leader, a winner, a king. And to do so you must go against what the majority does. The reason for this is that the majority are not leaders, winners, or kings. Therefore if you do what they do you will not end up as a leader, winner, or king. It is simple logic. Therefore you must go against them.

If the majority says that what you're doing is "dumb", "unpractical", or if they try to shame you then you know you're on the right path. This doesn't mean being dumb or unpractical or whatever means you're on the right path. No, what I mean is when people try to shame you through name calling of whatever type you're probably on to something. Sort of like hitting on women and them liking it makes you a "douchebag" to losers with no game or a pretty girl who gets male attention is automatically a "slut" to women who cannot compete with her. You get the idea. Go against the grain and you will be on your way to achieving freedom and becoming a king.

12 – Take Charge

You are the captain of your own ship. You have a crew with unquestioned loyalty. What you say they do. You are entirely responsible for where this ship ends up. You are after all the captain.

Most people are not aware of this. Most people act like they are first mates or deck swabs in their own ship. They let others dictate and decide where their ship ends up. Unfortunately their crew can't mutiny or bring their captain back to his rightful place because the captain holds all the power.

The ship is your life, the crew your mind, and the captain you. To get the ship where you want you must take the helm and direct your crew. Otherwise your ship will end up drifting aimlessly or worse crashing against the rocks.

It's all up to you, it's all on you. "What is?" you may ask. The answer is everything. Your life, the quality of it, the money you make, the women you date, the good you create in this world. It's all on you. You are the leader of your life whether you like it or not. It isn't a choice. There is no "I don't want to be a leader" option. There is only you're a good leader or a poor one.

This whole idea of third options handicaps many people. Like stated before good is more the opposite of great than bad is. People have this illusion that they can get by on okay and that as long as they keep their head down they'll never have to rise to the occasion. What they don't understand is that life doesn't give two shits what they think, it will bring the challenge to them and they better be ready or they will be crushed.

An army may have superior size and firepower yet if they meet another force with a better leader and more spirit they will get whipped. Look at the American

Civil War. The rebels had less men, technology, money, and everything else. However they had better leaders and a stronger belief in their ideals, add in fighting in their home territory and defending their families and they were almost able to defeat the northern forces. Yet on paper they weren't supposed to stand a chance.

I'm not here to make political commentary on the American Civil War simple to illustrate the difference that having strong leaders and a fighting spirit has. The same is true for your own life. Except you cannot rely on others to take the leadership role, it was given to you at birth.

Like a prince who was born to inherit the throne. He may not want it. He may hate the idea of having to lead and be a king but he has no option. Neither do you. To get what you want in life you must take actions to get it not wait on others.

Want to renew an old friendship? Then you must reach out. Want to have sex the beautiful woman sipping her coffee a few feet away from you? Then you must start the interaction and then lead it to where you want it to go. Things cannot be left to chance. Things drift towards chaos, not order. If you leave you yard untended will it become more beautiful or will it become overgrown and choked with weeds?

You must act on things to get them where you want to go. You are the actor, you are the force for you own life. Not chance, society, fate, others, or even God. He gave you that power and now expects you to do something with it.

If you only remember one thing from this book let it be this. *You are in control of your own life, where you end up is because of you.* It's all on you. To become a king is a choice. To be great, to rise above is a choice. A choice that it is up to you to make. Don't think there won't be consequences for ignoring this, there are. How many men leave this world unfulfilled and filled with regrets? How many men at their end truly feel that they did all that they could with the time that was given to them? Not many.

Don't be one of these men who die with their soul unfulfilled. Nothing is worth it. Like it says in the Bible "For what shall it profit a man, if he shall gain the whole world, and lose his own soul?". Your time and your mind are the most precious gifts that you have been given. Yet because they were given freely most people do not appreciate them.

    The most valuable things are free. Your time, your mind, the people you have relationships with. You can wipe out a man's riches yet he can get them back. You can destroy a man's empire and he can rebuild. However you destroy a man's mind and he is done. You waste his time and it can never be brought back. Yet how many people value a dollar over a minute? Which is more valuable? The minute is infinitely more valuable.

    The only way to get where you want and life is to lead yourself there. You are the king, the captain, the general. You can either be a great one that will be remembered for the ages or you can be one that never rises above the ranks of average.

Don't let this life pass you by. Don't waste a moment. Every second of your life should be directed towards a purpose. Every moment should bring you closer to your ultimate goals. Don't end up like the majority of men who die with their souls unfulfilled and realize it too late. Realize this now so that you can do something about it. It doesn't matter your age or anything else. Now is the time to seize the day and create the life of your dreams. Now is the time to go and take action, to be a leader. Because it is not a choice. The only choice is whether you will die angry, bitter, sad, and confused or satisfied with your life's work. Take the lead and seize the day.

13 – As You Think So Shall You Become

Our thoughts shape our reality. We become what we think about. What you think you create, what you feel you attract, and what you imagine you become. Think you are a loser and keep that thought in your mind and it will only be a matter of time before you are a loser. Your outer body reflects your inner thoughts. This doesn't just mean body fat percentages or muscle mass but how you carry yourself, your body language, your voice, and your smile. These things are reflections of how you think about yourself.

Think good positive thoughts about yourself and you will project that to the world. Think negative thoughts about yourself and that will also be projected to the world. Like most things in life this is a choice. You choose your thoughts or they can be chosen for you by society and others.

Your thoughts are habits of sorts. Think a negative thought a couple times and it's not going to do anything. Smoke a cigarette a few times and most likely it's not going to do anything to you. Negative thoughts become problems when you make a habit of them. When day in and day out you dwell on negative things and get stuck in that loop it will have a negative effect on your life. Likewise it's only when you smoke cigarettes day in and day out that your lungs start to take a beating. Repetition is what causes the effects for better or worse of your habits. One gym session won't do anything for you, it the consistency that will change your body.

Let's say we have two kids. We have James who was born into a small coal mining town. His father was a drunk and his mother depended on him for support and used him as her emotional crutch. He was the youngest of five brothers and often beaten up by them. He shares a bed with an older brother.

Then we have Thomas. Thomas was born into wealth. His dad is a rich banker and his mother a homemaker. An only child he has been spoiled his whole life. He has been given everything.

Both graduate from high school and now are on their way to the real world. During tenth grade James ran across a book written by a man named Earl Nightingale. He starts reading about how your thoughts shape your life. Being poor and beaten James has always had very low self-esteem and therefore works for minimum wage and has yet to kiss a girl. He thinks he is worthless but now determines to try and change it.

He talks to his family about it. His mother says "that's nice dear" and his brothers beat him for it. The book is destroyed in the process. Yet the idea is still there. Slowly James starts to change his thinking. He was struggling in school and thought about dropping out however now he decides to test out this theory on his school work. He graduates, barely, but he surprised his teachers and his parents even though they have other things on their mind.

James starts out as a door to door salesman. He barely makes a living but it is enough to separate him from his dysfunctional family and begin to grow healthily on his own.

Meanwhile Thomas goes to a private school and is given the best tutors. Thomas is naturally smart and is able to get through school no problem. He graduates and is automatically accepted at a large college. He pledges a fraternity he is a legacy at, his father is a large donor to the fraternity so they accept him. There he majors in business but spends most him time snorting coke and banging rich girls with daddy issues. He graduates and goes to work for his father.

    So to recap right now Thomas is far ahead of James. But things are about to change. Because of his positive mindset James takes every chance he has to grow. He soon becomes one of the best salesman in his field. Not only has he grown in business but also in self-development. Because he expects things to go well for him he is sleeping with a few beautiful women he has met. He finds he doesn't mind when they leave as his happiness isn't attached to them but found in himself, in his own mind.

Meanwhile Thomas gets fat and begins to hate himself. Though he wouldn't admit it and isn't aware of it, he hates himself for what he is. He knows others think lowly of him and think that he is a spoiled brat and in his rare moments of honesty Thomas knows that he is. Usually when he wakes up hungover with some tubby new hire. However Thomas is able to bury himself in making good money and sleeping with prostitutes and women that work for him.

James now thirty, he has built his own business that makes him money while he travels the world. He meets many different people and grows with every trip that he takes. He has met with others who run similar businesses across the world, he has climbed mountains in Asia, hunted big game in Africa, and explored the jungles of South America. He has an abundant sex life filled with beautiful women. He is even able to fund his own charity that helps tutor children with disabilities. James had made the most out of his life because of changing his mindset when he was in high school. He makes sure to buy a copy of Earl Nightingales book for every student that goes through his tutoring program and often gives speeches there when he is in town.

Thomas meanwhile continues in his cycle of getting fatter and sleeping with low self-esteem women. He knocked up a co-worker and a prostitute and now has to pay alimony for both. His father no longer talks to him though he lets him keep his job, as he knows Thomas will not be able to do anything else. Thomas looks at himself and hates who he has become. He has thought of suicide a couple of times and is deeply depressed.

What was the ultimate difference between these two? The reason why one ended up a success and the other a failure? Status?

Wealth? Starting position? No. The difference between these two was their thought life. Every advantage in the world will not help you if you have a negative thought life likewise every disadvantage in the world cannot hold you back if you have the right mindset. As you think so shall you become. This overrides everything. Money, looks, status, everything. It is imperative to your growth and development that you take control of your thought life. Don't try to make up for a deficiency in this through other ways. More money will not outweigh a negative mindset. Nothing will. Your mind creates your reality do not forget this.

14 – Eternal Growth

You must always keep learning. Let me repeat that. You must always keep learning. Forever. Growth is eternal. We've talked about this before but are going to further in depth in this chapter. To become king you must stand above the masses. You've heard the expression before that knowledge is power. To become a true king you must constantly seek out knowledge. Like a scholar after wisdom or a soldier after combat techniques and advantages. You should seek out new thought, knowledge, and ways of doing. As a king you must be well acquainted with all things. Relations between people, between sexes, knowledge of leadership, philosophy, business as well as how to build a healthy body and use it in the defense of that which you care about and much much more. As a king your growth is never complete.

    You must learn all that you can from the greats that came before you while also learning all the greats of the newest thought and ideas. You must be doing all of this while also filtering out all the B.S. that fills up so much of dominant thought. You must discriminate between that which is good and that which is not.

You must realize that there are people and groups who actively try to misinform and keep people dumb. I'm not necessarily talking about an Illuminati dark cult simply that those who are in power prefer it that way and a smart strong populace is a hindrance to that. It's not a conspiracy, it's common sense. The Romans had bread and circuses and we have football and reality TV. Principles don't change but their manifestations do.

    Test everything you read. Compare with different sources. This will take time but it ensures that you end up with good knowledge that will help you. Keep seeking out new knowledge and you picture of the world will become more and more complete. Never perfect, never entirely complete but closer. Therefore you will be able to make wiser decisions. This doesn't mean to postpone your decisions forever you still need to be decisive and always be moving forward. You must still take action. The point is to spend your time becoming more knowledgeable at things that matter in your life.

How to make money, have the sex life you want, be fulfilled in life, the right mindset to propel you to success. These are just some of the things that you must master to be a king. It goes far beyond this. This is just the beginning.

    When you look back at the greats that are remembered nearly every one of them dedicated themselves to acquiring knowledge and growing their entire lives. Until their deaths they were still learning, inventing, and trying. Think about these few examples. Socrates at age 80 the great Greek philosopher learned how to play a musical instrument. At age 88 Michelangelo designed the plans for the Church of Santa Maria Degli Angeli. At age 80 Johann von Goethe finished *Faust* considered to be his best work. And on the other side at age 3 Wolfgang

Mozart taught himself to play the harpsichord. At age 12 Carl von Clausewitz the famous author of *On War* joined the Prussian army. I could go on and on but the point is regardless of age these men continued to learn and grow. They never let it limit them.

They never thought "Oh I'm age X so therefore I can only do certain things". They had the proper mindset and are now known across the world as great men who accomplished much. Retirement from your career means nothing and honestly is something that will probably be phased out soon. With the way the economy and governmental tendencies are heading pensions and 401k type retirement plans will be a thing of the past. Many are finding that they do not have enough to retire and find that they must continue to work. While others retire and find that their life is now devoid of purpose. These people often grow old and die alone in a nursing home bitter and frustrated.

    Don't become one of these people. Being young is a choice. Not in biological age but in mental age. You can keep yourself sharp at any time and always should. A lot of you are probably thinking "That's great Charles I'll remember that in forty years however I'm 20, 30, or whatever. So how does this affect me?"

I'll tell you how. Despite being old these people were able to accomplish much. They didn't limit themselves so you being young why on earth would you limit yourself. You may think "I don't limit myself" but I call bullshit. We all limit ourselves in some way, shape, or form including me. It is something that we must fight against forever. Because every time we ascend to a new level there is always one higher. As I was saying, you say you don't limit yourself. Could you be a billionaire? "No, Charles of course not" why not? Perhaps you don't have a desire to be a billionaire but don't tell me you can't be. Look Bill Gates is human, every billionaire that has ever lived has been human. So you may not desire to ever have a billion and that is just fine but don't lie and say you'll never be a billionaire because it isn't possible. It is entirely possible.

Another example. Maybe you're vacationing in Miami and you see a famous celebrity or a Victoria Secret model. You are incredibly attracted to her but you don't say anything because you figure she wouldn't be interested.

You say "They only sleep with men who are rich or famous" but this is again a limiting thought. They are human who sleep with other humans and by putting them on a pedestal in your mind you will never sleep with them. What I'm getting at is that you do limit yourself. We all do. You have to learn to overcome this.

I'm not saying that just walking around saying "I can be a billionaire" will net you billions. You obviously have to take action. What I'm saying is that if you conclude you could never be a billionaire you insure one hundred percent that you never will be. Most people limit themselves a lot more than the examples above. Some feel they can never make a million or some guys think that they couldn't even get a girlfriend. This is ridiculous.

Acquire knowledge, cultivate the right mindset, and then take action. That's the summary of success. That is what I want you to take away from this chapter.

15 – Beliefs Govern Behavior

Your actions were all at one time thoughts. Everything that you do, you do for a reason. Even if you are not aware of that reason. The beliefs that you have deep in your subconscious mind are what govern your behavior. The thoughts deep in your mind are the reasons for why you do the things you do and why you act the way that you act.

To become a king you must adapt the beliefs of a king. Now you may ask what are the beliefs of a king? There are many but there are a select few that I want you to focus on in this chapter. The first is that a king is deserving of good things. The second is that a king naturally leads, he doesn't mind being in charge. The third is that a king is a fighter and does not bow down to others. The forth is that a king has goals and a mission in life. The fifth is a king is wise.

Deserving of Good Things

People feel that if bad things happen to them then that makes them more noble than if good things were to happen to them. This is foolish thinking. You are not better because bad things happen to you. Having bad things happen to you does not make you morally superior to others. If anything it means you are fool if bad things continually happen to you. It means you're not adjusting and doing something wrong. If someone ran his head into a wall time and time again what would you think of this person? That he is worthy of respect for continually going through what he is going through? Or that he is an idiot?

Yet when it comes to other situations people are given sympathy when it does nothing but insure they will never rise above their situations. Someone goes from bad relationship to bad relationship and people feel so sorry he or she "can't find a good partner". If someone is on their fourth or fifth marriage it's probably them that's the problem not all the "bad men" or "lying women".

There is nothing noble about being a loser. There is nothing noble about being poor and destitute. There is nothing noble about being weak. You deserve good things. When someone pays you a compliment don't deny it, accept it. If someone told me I was great my response would either be "I know" or "Thank you". You may think that is cocky but that is the right attitude to have. That is the attitude of a king.

You should accept when good things happen to you. Do not fight them. If a beautiful women wants to sleep with you accept that as normal. When you start making more money in a month than you previously made in a year accept it. Bad things are not supposed to happen to you. Sure some will but you should seek out good things. Do not be one of those people who deny good things because they think it's noble. It isn't noble, it's stupid.

Natural Leader

Kings are comfortable in the front. Being in the lead. They don't feel bashful about it, they feel that it is their rightful place. This is an attitude you must adapt. Don't be timid, don't be shy. Winners are natural leaders. When things need to be done they take the lead and get things done. They don't wait on others, they don't outsource their life issues or problems. When something is wrong they address it.

Think of this example. You are treated disrespectfully while out in public. Someone cuts in front of you in line. Most people would react in one of two ways. Become aggressive or become timid. They would either let it pass or freak out about it causing a scene. Whereas a leader would address the problem in a direct assertive way and would be prepared to back up every word that he said. You've probably heard the expression "Never start a fight but always finish one" this is the mindset of a leader. They don't go out looking for trouble but they solve problems when they do come up.

Be A Fighter

Cowards do not get far in life. This has been true since the dawn of mankind and it is true today. While you may not die nowadays for being a coward like you would in the past, it will still hold you back tremendously.

When I say be a fighter, I don't mean a jackass who goes around looking for a fight. Someone who is always talking crap and causing trouble. This is the mark of someone who is insecure and generally has never been in a real fight. Because if they had they wouldn't be looking for one. When someone acts like this you can safely bet they are all bark and no bite.

What I mean by being a fighter is being someone who doesn't give in. Someone who stands by their beliefs even if they are unpopular. Who will stand their ground when others are against them. Don't get me wrong sometimes being a fighter will mean physically fighting. Whether it is for country, belief, or self-respect but more often than not it means taking a stand.

Kings do not go around apologizing for holding unpopular beliefs. They do not bend over every time someone tells them that they should, every time someone challenges their beliefs. They do not care if others hate or dislike them. They have no problem trampling over the sacred cows and beliefs of the sheep. Not for the sake of disrespecting them but because they are loyal to the truth and their ideals. Be a fighter, do not back down from your ideals or beliefs.

Your Mission

Kings know in what direct they want to go in. They have an overall picture of their kingdom. What they want it to be, how they want it to grow. A future vision of what they want. Put another way kings have goals. Goals that they do not deviate from. Goals that they set out to achieve every day. Goals that they do not give up on.

Kings are persistent in striving towards their goals. They do productive activities every day that lead them closer to the achievement of their goals. They do waste their times with the activities of the masses. When they have fun, they have fun and when they work, they work hard.

Because of this they are able to strike a balance. They are able to enjoy the good times more than the average person. Because of the hard work they have done to accomplish their goals when they have fun, they do not have a weight over their head worrying about other things. As they have taken action to rise up from their problems and have gone after the life that they want.

The Cultivation of Wisdom

Kings spend time cultivating wisdom and knowledge. We talked about this before but it bears repeating. Kings place a premium on wisdom. They value it more than gold, because it is in fact more valuable than gold. Wisdom will get you anywhere.

Take away everything a man has but that man can build it all back because of wisdom. Like Benjamin Franklin said "If a man empties his purse into his head no one can take it away from him. An investment in knowledge always pays the best interest." Remember this quote. I would suggest writing it down until it becomes a part of you.

Wisdom is something that takes time to grow completely. However like the oak tree once fully grown it is incredibly strong and stable.

Wisdom is the strongest foundation. It will lead to wealth, health, and happiness.

Your beliefs govern your behavior. We covered a few beliefs here but there are many more that makeup the mindset of a king. Cultivate healthy beliefs. Beliefs that work for you instead of against you. Change your beliefs and your behavior will follow. Strike at the cause instead of at the symptom. Put another way you can spend all day hacking at the branches of a tree and you will get nowhere. However when you strike at the roots, at the foundation then everything changes.

16 – Have Hustle

Having hustle does not mean cheating or robbing people of their money. Having hustle means being a go getter. Someone who gets things done and works hard. Having hustle means being someone who isn't afraid to put the work in to get to where they want to get to.

Many people avoid work like it's the plague. They seek every loophole they can to do the least amount of work as possible. This person is doing themselves a disservice and will never rise above the level of mediocrity. I'm sure you've heard plenty of friends moaning about living paycheck to paycheck but at the same time not doing anything about it.

Someone who has hustle doesn't really care about the hours worked but about the end goal. Hustlers don't mind working weekends, nights, or whenever else to get to where they want to go. They are about getting work done and producing not about cutting corners.

Now some of you probably have this idea in your mind of a hustler as that young guy who puts in a bunch of extra hours at the office. You know the first one there and last one out, barely has time for family or friends. Usually works for a domineering boss, etc. You get the idea. This is not a hustler. This is a slave. Hustlers focus on their own work. It is idiotic to sacrifice your time and life for someone else (such as your corporate boss) and expect them to appreciate you for it. They will use and abuse you then discard you like yesterday's trash. Because that is how they see you, as being expendable, as being trash. Hustlers work for themselves, they dedicate their time to building their own brand and business.

    Let's use a story to illustrate the difference. We have Rick and Michael who both work for Corporation X. They both worked hard in high school and college, graduated with honors and are now working for a reputable company. In addition to working for the same company both Michael and Rick have side businesses.

    Michael gets in early and stays late. He is always at the beck and call of his boss Ron. He knows Ron is a complete ass but also wants to excel in the company. Michael gets home exhausted. During the week he is too tired to work on his business so saves it for weekends. However he usually spends his weekends going out to relieve all the stress from the week leaving a few hours during the day to build his business.

Lately Ron has asked Michael to start coming in weekends as well. Michael accepts this as he has dedicated his life to this job.

    Rick meanwhile works at the same business and in the same position. He does work when asked but avoids any extra work like the plague. He knows he probably won't advance but he was never good at kissing ass anyways. When he gets home he spends an hour every night working on his business. During the weekends he doesn't always go out as he doesn't need the stress relief because he lives a balanced life. However occasionally he does go out for fun. Rob has asked Rick to come in weekends but Rick refused. Rob warned Rick that this could cost him his job Rick said he's okay with this. After a few months of this Rick gets fired. Rick has to downsize and give up his nice apartment downtown. However he makes enough money from his side business to not have to look for a job.

    Rick takes advantage of this and devotes his time completely to expanding his business. He puts in some applications but isn't too concerned if they go through or not. Rick dedicates his life to himself. After a year he is able to build his business to the point he is making as much as he did in his corporate job. But with a major exception. He enjoys and loves what he is doing.

Meanwhile Michael was passed over for a promotion by this new hire. He worked harder than her, had seniority over her, and she hadn't even been working weekends. Michael wasn't sure if it was a Feminist initiative, she was sleeping with Rob, or what but he does know this. He has wasted a large chunk of his life for nothing. Sure over time perhaps he'll progress or maybe not. Michael goes home exhausted and stressed. He sleeps poorly, is getting fatter, and barely has time to have a relationship or a good sex life. He realizes that this could very well be his entire life. He has dedicated himself to something outside of himself which will never give him the returns he desires. He saw Rick the other day. Despite being fired Rick seemed happy and at peace. Michael begins devoting himself to him own business.

    There is a difference between being busy and being productive. Likewise there is a difference between working your ass off and being a hustler. An ox can work his ass off but he can never be a hustler. Weird analogy but bear with me. Being a hustler requires intelligence. It's not mindlessly slaving away. It's working hard but with an intelligent purpose. It's not being busy, it's being productive.

Some people think the more stressed and on edge they are, the better they are doing. This is stupid. Being on edge and stressed are not good things. You can work hard without being stressed or on edge. This, like the "if bad things happen to me I'm a good person" paradigm is utter horseshit. People get stuck in all these weird loops. The victim mentality is a cancer, it is poison to the soul of man. It keeps people from achieving greatness because they associate goodness with being a loser. There is nothing noble about being a loser.

    Work hard and work smart. Have hustle and be productive. There isn't a choice between working hard or working smart you must be doing both to the best of your ability. Otherwise you won't ever get off the ground.

17 – Never Compromise

Compromising is no virtue. We're often told that compromise is a good thing, when the truth of the matter is that compromise is more often a bad thing. Compromise means giving up on your beliefs, it means settling. Two things kings have no intention of doing. We're taught in modern society that it is noble to give up your beliefs that to stand firm in your beliefs makes you close minded or a bigot. It's a shaming technique. Like calling a guy a "fag" if he tries something new. It stems from peoples own insecurities and ironically their own close mindedness.

    Compromising the truth with a lie simply hurts the truth. The middle is not always correct. As a matter of fact those who are lukewarm are perhaps the ones who are most often in the wrong. Look at it this way let's say you get relationship advice from three people. Me, your friend who has been in a long term relationship since high school, and an angry Feminist. Obviously we are all going to be saying different things. So what the "open minded" person would do is compromise all three things said. Would this do him any favors? Hell no, it would simply distort my message with watered down or completely wrong bullshit. Instead of taking the full truth he would take a half measure of the truth and mix it with lies.

Let me ask you a question if you were given a glass of Maker's Mark (or whatever your favorite bourbon is), a glass of dirty dish water, and a glass of gasoline. Would you be better off taking a sip from each or just drinking the Maker's Mark? Would you be closed minded to say no I'm only going to drink the Maker's Mark because it is the best? The average Westerner would believe that he must drink from all three. This type of thinking is insane at best and entirely destructive at worst.

There is a hierarchy for everything. For example in the universe there is the hierarchy of God, angels, man, then beasts and we could take it even lower than that. There is a natural order to the universe. Don't think you have to give every idea or person the time of day because you don't. Most ideas and people out there are crap. This may not sound nice but it is the truth. Most of what you hear is garbage and most people are way off path and misled. Again this doesn't mean to hate them but to ignore them.

One area where modern man is told to compromise the most is in his relationships. And by compromise meaning do whatever the hell the woman wants whenever the hell she wants it. You shouldn't compromise in your relationships in the traditional sense of the world much less the modernized version described above.

Remember compromising truth for lies does not make the truth better. Compromising winning for losing does not make winning better. Compromising leads to weak ideas ascending over strong. Compromise leads to all ideas being equal. The very worst with the very best. Imagine if parents compromised, though you might not have to imagine this as this trend has taken off in Western society. The opinions of the parents equal with the opinions of their children. The top ten percent of society's opinions equal with the lowest ten percent of society's opinions. Isaac Newton's and Max Planck's opinions equal with that of the latest Feminist/Marxist professor living off taxpayers dollars.

Compromise leads to the destruction of good, of strength, and of beauty. Do not take part in this evil. Stand firm in the truth and in the light. Do not compromise your wisdom with the foolishness of the world. Do not compromise your light with the darkness. Do not compromise your truth with lies.

If I compromised I would have never gotten to the point I am at now. For example when I started researching how to make money online I knew absolutely no one who did this. Everyone around me thought it wasn't tenable and honestly at first I agreed with them. Yet after further research and then testing I found that running a website and writing books was something that could not only give a man an income to live off of but also give him the freedom to explore the world and do as he pleased.

    Yet others still doubted this. I had people close to me say I needed to focus on getting "a real job" which apparently translates to "A job and life you hate". I could have compromised and said "Alright I'll do the website and book thing on the side but focus on my career" instead I ignored them and focused on my own path. Because I know better than them. That's right I know better than them. Again most people think that this sounds cocky. But it is the truth. I know what path my own life should take better than others do. I did not leave the path and that has made all the difference.

I do not compromise and it insures that I remain on the right path. It doesn't matter if you are religious or not there is much wisdom to be found in the religious books. In the Bible Jesus goes out in the desert to fast for forty days. There Satan tempts and tests him. Satan offers him many different things if he would just compromise. Nowadays Satan would say "don't be such a bigot" and "stop being so closed minded" or "you're such an X, Y, or Z". Jesus rebuked Satan and continued on his path. The path that he knew was right for him. The path that many others including at times his disciples tried tempting him out of. Yet Jesus knew he had a purpose and did not let others dissuade him from his path. Jesus rejected the evils of compromise.

    You can learn a lot from that story. Stick firm to your beliefs. Do not be swayed and whatever you do, do not compromise. Compromising good with evil does not make you open minded, it makes you evil. Compromising truth with lies does not make you noble or good or open minded, it makes you a liar. Stand firm, be a man, be a king and always remember. Never compromise.

18 – Be Positive

If there is one thing that I cannot stand it is whining or negativity. People who make excuses. The excuses change with the ages but the effect they have remains the same. They divorce people from their own responsibility for their life so that they can blame others. These people don't want to achieve their dreams they want others to feel bad for them, they want to be lazy.

Negativity can be just as debilitating. I should start by addressing the opposite of negative, positivity. In particular what positivity is. As most people have a warped concept of what it means to be positive or an optimist.

When the word positivity or optimism comes to mind most people think of cheesy motivational sayings or people with fake smiles plastered on their faces who are always in a good mood. This isn't true positivity. This is fake. This isn't real. This is a thin veneer over something else. True positivity is something that radiates from the inside. People who are truly positive do not subscribe to a Pollyanna world view or have the outlook of a naïve child but are instead realists. Don't think cheesy corporate sayings or motivation speakers are what I am talking about when I say to be positive. What I am saying is to not whine or complain but to take things in stride and expect good things to happen. Alright now that we know what I mean by being positive we can get into how to avoid negativity.

Whining, complaining, excuse making these are all habits of the masses, of losers. They are all habits that cripple and debilitate people from living the lives that they want. They divorce people from their responsibilities and cause them to look for help outside of themselves. They blame God, society, others, an assorted mix of isms, and anything else that they can. This mindset is poison to the accomplishment of your goals and dreams.

 Negativity is the default mode of society. Because of this you must be extra diligent in fighting against it. It is human nature to see the bad over the good. To see the problem over the opportunity. Which is why so many people end up stuck and stagnate. Because they always see the glass as being half-empty. It gets to the point where even when opportunity is staring them right in the face they cannot see it.

 Here is an example. Let say we have a guy named Bill. Bill thinks that girls don't like him and that they never will. He thinks that girls only like guys with X, Y, or Z. None of which Bill has. Let's pause for a moment and take a look at Bill's line of thinking. First off he declares that "girls" do not like him. There are 3.52 billion women on this planet, of those there is a guarantee that some will like him. You see this how ridiculous this statement is. Let's say this way of thinking started in high school when Bill got stood up a couple of times. So now he's let a few (or one) negative interaction turn into an entire mindset.

    Regardless let's continue. When Bill goes out he's not women's first choice and he doesn't approach women because again "girls won't like me". Most nights he doesn't talk to women and they don't talk to him. This is Bill's own fault for not taking action, having a bad mindset, and a million other reasons but he doesn't see this. He sees it as being outside of himself. Anyways one night for whatever reason a girl comes up and starts talking to Bill. She is interested in Bill and attracted to him. Bill talks to her but then at the end of the nights gets up and walks away from her to go home. His friends say "Bill what the hell are you doing? That girl was into you" but Bill responds with "That isn't possible". The reason Bill says this is because Bill has focused on the women who didn't want him in his life and has drawn out false conclusions from the few bad interactions he had. His mindset won't allow for the possibility that a woman may like him or find him attractive. It clashes too deeply with his beliefs that he has ingrained into himself.

Perhaps some of you feel sorry for Bill. Don't, it is Bill's own damn fault for where he is and pitying him will do nothing but keep him there. Bill chose to focus on the negatives (along with having a host of other issues) and it cost him and it always will. There is a cost to every mindset we adapt, every action we take, and every thought we think. This can be good or bad depending on many factors but one thing remains constant. That there is a cost.

Bill was just one example. There are millions of other ways in which people let their negative thinking dictate their lives and careers. It goes far beyond just sleeping with women.

Let's use another example. Now let's say we have Jack. Jack has a positive mindset and has been through even more than Bill. During high school his girlfriend he had since ninth grade cheated on him with his best friend. Then the next girl he dated dumped him on prom night to get banged by her friend's older brother. In college he decided to take his dating life into his own hands and begin going out meeting women. He asked a few acquaintances of friends out on dates and was rejected by all of them. Senior year of college he finally was able to take a woman home with him but she passed out in his bed. At this point Jack has had a crappier sex life then ninety-nine percent of men out there. He is on the course to become the real life forty year old virgin.

 But Jack shrugs it off and continues on. After graduation he is able to sleep with a coworker. It was a onetime thing but whatever at this point Jack is taking what he can get. He has forgotten his negative experiences and remembers this one. He goes out and because he has positive expectations and a positive attitude has more and more success with women. It gets to the point that by the time Jack is twenty five all his friends can't believe how many women are constantly blowing up his phone and hitting on him.

You're probably not as bad as Jack and even if you are or were you can still get out of any situation you are in with the right mindset. A mindset of positivity. What you focus on increases. So focus on the good, focus on the positive. This doesn't mean being a naïve child, it means being smart while also having an optimistic outlook on life. Life can always get better and it can always get worse. The choice is yours to make. Be positive and make life better for you every day.

19 – Chart Your Own Path

You are unique. Though there are similar traits that you share will all human beings ultimately you are unique. The combination of your thoughts, dreams, and desires is unique. What makes you fulfilled and happy will be different from what makes me fulfilled and happy in some way, shape, or form. Sure we probably both want money, women, health, and many other things but what that looks like to each of us may be different.

For example some of us want to have a small amount of money but earn it in a way that they are able to travel around the world. While some others want to acquire vast sums so that they can live in New York or some other city they have dreamed about. Then there are others who want large sums of money but only want a medium sized home but want to never have to worry about money and donate to a charity that they care deeply about. So you see all of these goals deal with money. They all have to do with acquiring a certain amount of money. One person may be miserable being stuck in one city while another would be miserable traveling the world. People are different. Because of this your path to ultimate fulfillment, to living the life of your dreams, to becoming a king. Is going to be different from anyone else who has ever lived.

    Look at it like this. Imagine you and I were both required to write a book about a man living in Alaska. Though we were given the same assignment what that book will look like and be about is going to be completely different. Again of course there will be similarities. No matter what our ultimate goal may be the path to achieving it will require learning, hard work, and dedication. But the manifestation will be different.

    You are going to have to go your own way at some point. Others can give you guidance and advice. Others can show you the principles that will lead you to where you want to go. But you are the one who has to take action to get there. You must take the action, you must have confidence in yourself and go. The path ahead of you will be untracked and potentially filled with danger and adventure. You will have to go where you feel uncomfortable. You will have to go where you feel afraid. When you feel scared, when you feel unsure of yourself, you know that you are in uncharted territory and on the right path.

 Think about the explorers who came over from Europe to explore the new world. No one knew what they would find when they reached the other side. But the potential for riches, fame, and adventure propelled them across the sea. There some found gold and others death. Some found happiness and others destruction. They thrill of adventure and risk was enough to entice more and more to come over.

    Today we may not have an uncharted continent to explore. But there are plenty of adventures to be had and trails to be blazed. Starting a business is an adventure. If you work for someone else you are never going to get rich. Only by setting out on your own and developing your own brand can you ever hope to make the money you want. Sure there is potentially more risk setting out on your own than remaining in the comforts of your job but the rewards are also greater. You may say "most businesses fail" and you would be right. But most businesses are started by normal people. Are you a normal person? Remember normal is not a compliment if anything it is an insult. If you were normal you would not be reading this book. If you were normal you would be watching sports, watching mindless videos on the internet, or surfing the latest social networking site seeing what was happening in the lives of others.

Just like when men came over from Europe to the Americas. The ones who were not hardened and fighting men usually died out. But the ones who were leaders, warriors, and prepared were often the ones who returned home with riches or fame. Being uncomfortable is good. It is a sign you are doing something new and because of that you are expanding and growing.

When you see a drop dead gorgeous women enter a room and go and talk to her, you grow. When you start you own business and expand it, you grow. When you feel fear but still act, you grow. By growing you will grow into your own unique path. You will become what it is that you want to be.

I'll use an example from my own life. Most people's biggest fear is speaking in public. I remember in high school getting nervous before giving a presentation in front of the class. However while also nervous after doing it I felt good. Especially since I generally over prepared to quell the nervousness and ended up doing a pretty good job. It got to the point where I would volunteer to be the one who lead the presentation and do the most talking. I took speech in college and enjoyed it. I soon found that this transferred into many other areas of my life.

An even earlier example would be working out. I started lifting weights in the eighth grade. I remember watching others older than me bench one thirty five and thought that would be impossible for me. I struggled with a few tens on the bar. I was unsure of myself when I got under the bar. Yet after consistent effort was able to slowly and surely make gains. To the point where I excelled past all those that I looked up to before.

These things, along with many others, helped shape me into the man I am today. They helped shape me into the man that is able to blaze my own trail and follow my own path. While I listen to the advice of others who I respect ultimately I make my decisions for me and know that if something feels right to me I should do it. Even if others say I shouldn't or if others have failed. I know my path is unique and I can either chart it and contribute something new and unique to the world or I can let fear hold me back from ever exploring my own trail and dying unfulfilled.

20 – Self-Education

There is only one true form of education and that is self-education. Degrees, certificates, and awards are nice and all but they have little meaning when compared to self-education and those three things are often done more to make a statement or for a business to make money off of you than anything. For example for most people college is going to be a waste of money. It will sink them further in debt and do little to help get them to a better station in life. At one time colleges were a place of learning and worth the investment. This is no longer the case. Another prime example is personal training certifications. To work in a big box gym, not that you ever would as becoming you own brand is a one hundred times better option, you have to be certified by certain boards. These certifications cost one thousand dollars on the low end and teach you ineffective methods. They focus on being risk free and water down political correct B.S., they will never get anyone strong or healthy. Yet people signup every day to dump their money into these courses.

    True expertise comes from experience and learning about something yourself. If I wanted to learn about history about the worst thing I could do is go to history class. Whether it is in college or high school. It's still watered down and politically correct and even if it wasn't you still have to deal with the limitations of the teacher or professor. No, if you want to learn about something you go to the source. You go to someone you know who knows what they are doing or you read books from the leaders of that particular field.

  The number one place where you can truly be educated is the library. Grab some pens and a notepad then head over. The library is filled with more knowledge than any of your professors, teachers, and relatives. And this would still be true even if our education system wasn't such a joke. You don't go to school to learn. You go to school because it's mandated. School for the most part is a waste of time. Once you learn reading, writing, and basic arithmetic you're better off going out on your own and learning.

Your time is too valuable of a resource to waste rotting away in the education system. Along with your mind it is your most valuable resource. Which also rots away in the education system. Education in the traditional sense means nothing, while self-education means everything. Self-education is often the difference between success and failure. Between greatness and obscurity. Look back at the greats of history, how many of them got to where they were because of their education? How many of them got to where they were because of their self-education? Most people who stay in the education system end up being strangled by it. Their creative thought is strangled and their risk taking attitude lost. The education system is great at producing cogs or sheep. Not producing men.

Give me a man who has a doctorate in a subject and give me a man who has read one hundred books on a subject through his own study and I will take the man who read the one hundred books on his own time any day of the week. Unless you are a doctor or lawyer, staying in education is going to be a waste of your time. And even then don't think because you are a doctor or lawyer you are going to have it made because you aren't. Believe it or not but there are plenty of struggling doctors and lawyers, and that's without adding in the debt they acquired from their schooling.

The purpose of education is to come to the understanding of new knowledge. To further your own development. It is something that you must take responsibility for. It is something that you must work at personally. Teachers, preachers, and loved ones will all mislead you. And when you end up somewhere you didn't want to, you will have no one to blame but yourself for not taking matters into your own hands. Traditional schooling if anything hampers the development of your mind and the hippy alternatives are even worse.

If you want to be educated, and by educated I mean truly educated. Not have a wall of degrees, a mountain of debt, and think all the "right" thoughts educated but really educated than you best bet is books, the library, and people you know who are ahead in the field of your study.

    Here is what I would do. I think everyone on this earth should have their own personal library. Regardless of their age, race, gender, occupation, religion, or anything else. Listen to what Andrew Carnegie the richest man of his generation had to say about libraries "A library outranks any other one thing a community can do to benefit its people. It is a never failing spring in the desert". Wouldn't it be nice to have your own spring in your own home? Everything you have ever wanted to know is out there. Every problem that you have has a solution. It may not be an easy solution or the one you want to hear but it has a solution nonetheless. Of all the many things that I have done in my life there is few that have benefitted me more than devoting myself to the reading and studying of good books.

Good books can open your mind to things you never thought about and never would have thought about. They can shave months or years or even decades off of your learning time. They make easy for you what was hard for others. Books have incredible value in them. They are more valuable than gold. Like the great king Solomon says in the book of Proverbs "How much better is it to get wisdom than gold. And to get understanding rather than choice silver." Solomon was also the richest man of his time. You may notice but there tends to a correlation between quality of life and wisdom. So go out and start your own personal library. You own fountain of wisdom.

21 – Limiting Beliefs

One of my favorite quotes is by Henry Ford he said "Whether you think you can or think you can't, you're right". What Ford was talking about is your beliefs decide where you are going to go. If you think you'll never be rich then it is a one hundred percent guarantee that you will never be rich. Your beliefs can act like a governor (speed limiter) in a car. You will never go past your beliefs. If you believe you can only bench press a certain amount then you will never go beyond that amount. Your mind which is in control of your body won't let you. It works the same way for everything else in life.

So many people have limiting beliefs. The beliefs have been put there by the usual culprits' society, parents, "education", etc. but are also put there by the individual himself. You are in control of your thoughts and you are in control of your beliefs. It makes no sense to limit yourself.

For example let's say you were competing in a marathon. And let's say that the winner of this marathon will get one million dollars, second place half a million, third a quarter million, and so on and so forth for the first ten places. Now let's say you have prepared for the marathon and been working hard for months or even years to get to the position that you are in now. You're properly hydrated, warmed up, and well fed. The gun fires and the race is off (or however marathons start). You start out. An outside observer would notice something strange about this marathon namely that everyone is using only one leg. You included. So we have a race that you have been given all the right equipment for, that you are prepared for, and that has a great reward at the end yet everyone is only using one leg. This doesn't make sense right?

Life is the same way except worse. People use a lot less than fifty percent of what they are capable of and the rewards of life are infinitely greater than one million dollars. It's most likely then when you looked at the marathon example you thought all those people were fools yet if you looked at your own life you're probably just as guilty. I know I was. Does this make us fools? No, not at all. However after becoming aware of our limiting beliefs and then not doing anything about it would make us fools.

It's one thing to error because of ignorance but then to continue in error after knowing the correct way is something completely different. For example when I was young if I bumped into someone I was taught to say "excuse me". When a kid bumps into someone unless their having a particular bad day or feel like being an ass they won't have much of a reaction. However if an adult goes around and bumps into people it is completely different. He will at best get dirty looks but might also get hit.

    I want you to think about any limiting beliefs that you may have. Most have limiting beliefs about money, dating/who they sleep with, and their own development as a person. I want you to get rid of those beliefs by letting go of them and letting reality dictate where you end up. This like everything else is a process. The first key though is to be aware that you have limiting beliefs, identifying them, and then recognizing that they are limiting and not healthy for your development.

For example most guys have a limiting belief in regards to what women will be attracted to them and when they will have sex with them. For example I've seen guys who think that a girl won't have sex before three dates. Whereas depending on a couple of factors some women will have sex within three minutes. Other guys think that attractive girls only like guys with money, fame, or looks. While there is no denying that women are attracted to these things there is much more to the story. Beautiful women sleep with men who don't have fame, looks, or money all of the time. These men are assigning themselves to a lower level of life than they are capable of. They are voluntarily putting themselves in their own self-made prisons. Prisons that they all have the key for.

    The story of the elephant and the rope is a perfect example of this. A young elephant was brought into a circus from the African savanna. He was tied to a post with a rope. The elephant struggled and fought day and night for months to break free from the rope but it never broke. Eventually the elephant gave up. Years later the same elephant now fully grown is led around by that small rope and tethered to the same post with it. The elephant could snap the rope with little effort yet it has been conditioned that the rope is stronger than him. Yet all the elephant would have to do is tug slightly and the rope would snap and he would be free.

 A lot of people are like that elephant and in a number of ways.

When young they were told this or that and it became their beliefs. Sometimes it was for their own good but much more likely it was done with ulterior motives. Ulterior motives that are not in your best interest or even in your interest at all. The biggest roadblock and asset to success is your own mind. It is the beginning and the end.

Take the mind of a genius and place it into a completely different body with a completely different brain and change any factor you want. Height, race, sex, class, or whatever and that mind will take that body to greatness. Every time. It's like when you see a millionaire lose everything but then become a millionaire again a few years later while the majority of people grind away barely getting by in that same period of time. That's because it is all about the person's mindset and their beliefs. Successful people get rid of limiting beliefs. They let reality decide where they fall not the smallness of their own beliefs. Get out of your own way. Don't limit yourself. Don't go one hundred when the speed limit is infinite. Don't hop on one leg when you can run on two. Get rid of your limiting beliefs and watch yourself accelerate beyond what you ever thought possible.

22 – Action Creates Momentum

Starting something worthwhile is often like a snowball rolling downhill. When your first set out to do something worthwhile. Whether it may be starting a business, improving yourself, writing and selling a book, or whatever the beginning is generally the hardest part. It's like starting a snowball. You have to grab the snow and pack it together yourself. Then once the snowball is big enough that it won't fall apart is when you can begin to roll it down a hill. Once the snowball starts rolling down the hill it will pick up more and more snow. Eventually the snowball will get big enough that is will grow to the point where it can't be stopped. It will pick up speed and size at an exponential rate. What started with your action of creating a snowball ended up being continued on by the momentum of the snowball.

 Let's say you set out to write a book. You research the topic, take what you've learned in your own life, and then test and refine that to make sure your readers are getting the best information possible. This step can take quite some time if done properly. Or if you are already an expert in your subject you can begin right away. You then outline the topics that you want to cover and once that is done you begin actually writing the book. Once the book is written which generally takes a while you then have to edit and revise it. After that you format it and publish it.

Once published you then have to start marketing it and getting it in front of people. Most authors never get past this part and their book remains unseen and eventually fades away. However once it starts catching on it has the potential to begin rolling downhill. Someone reads it and tells their friend about it.

This goes on for a couple of months. A couple sites write reviews about it. You start getting more and more personal reviews for it. Fast forward three years later it is a best seller that makes you lots of money and has a positive effect on many people.

This all started because you took action. The momentum would have never gathered if you had not taken action. You must act upon your life to change it. Objects in rest will stay at rest unless acted on by an outside force. You must be the ignition, the spark that starts the blaze. When you keep at something long enough at some point it may take off to the point where you don't have to worry about it but that takes time and effort.

A prime example of this is raising the young. Most animals take care of their young to the point where they have a chance of making it on their own. Think of the book example above. At first it took lots of work with little reward then with time it takes on a life of its own. Do you think the author of bestsellers have to market their books nearly as hard as before once they become bestsellers? Of course not. The book has taken on a life of its own and now grows without the input and guidance of the author. The author's action has created the momentum.

Think of planting a tree. The seed could be easily crushed or destroyed. In the beginning the tree requires protection and nurturing. Even as a sapling it is still weak and can easily be destroyed by the forces of man or nature. But once that tree reaches a certain point it becomes strong enough that it doesn't have to be taken care of. It can withstand just about whatever is thrown at it.

You have the power to create. By taking action you put things in motion. It will take time and effort but by consistently taking action you put things in motion. You may not see it, some never realize it no matter how successful they get, but rest assured that something is happening. For every cause there is an effect for every action there is an equal and opposite reaction. These laws cannot be denied. They can work for you or against you, but they cannot be denied. It is up to you to take the right actions to create the right momentum. Whether it is building a business that goes on to change the lives of millions for the better or whether it is taking that first hit of meth and ending up broke and a drug addict. It works both ways.

    The world works in certain ways. Certain laws govern it. You can break yourself against these laws or you can harness them to propel you far above the level of the average man. To greatness, to riches, to kingship.

When you first take action you never know what the reaction will ultimately be. Smiling at a beautiful women could end up being a marriage. Taking a wrong turn could be the end of your life. Writing that book could be the thing that brings you and your family riches. Starting that website could the thing that keeps a man from killing himself. You never know what is going to happen, you need to take action. Go and take action and understand that there will be a reaction. And if you are taking good action there will be a good reaction. Though this doesn't mean the reaction will be pleasant.

For example you may write something that is the truth but it offends people. So you are attacked labeled a variety of words and come under a lot of pressure. You may see this as being punished for taking right action but it is not. First off like they say in show business "There is no such thing as bad publicity", when you get attention you are furthering the reach of your message. Second you are exposing peoples lies either lies they have been told or lies that they are telling. This causes a reaction in them. This is good. Just because they react negatively to it doesn't mean it isn't good for them. Sometimes people need harsh truths to break their pleasant delusions that will only lead them to more suffering ultimately. It may suck to tell someone their spouse has been sleeping with others and they may even get mad at you for telling them but ultimately it is for their best that you do so. Right action leads to right reaction, though it may not be pleasant.

23 – Importance of Solitude

We are under constant stimulation in the modern world. Through the internet, TV, ads, and much more. There is hardly a time or place when a man can be alone with his thoughts. This is unfortunate. As solitude is one of the best things for a man to develop his thinking capacities, his own self-image, and be alone with his thoughts. Solitude is paramount to your full development. Throughout the ages the wisest men have wandered in the wilderness or set up a study so that they could be alone with their thoughts, without the distractions of the world. There are many men who live their entire lives under constant stimulation. From work, spouse, children, others, and the media.

Solitude is important for a number of reasons, namely. Clearness of thought, to reconnect with yourself, and focus on life goals. Each will be dealt with in turn.

Clearness of Thought

It is not impossible for a man to go his entire day without thinking. To go his entire day without thinking a true thought. What goes on in his head are reactions.

Reactions to the world around him, not true thought. Going to sleep a man's mind can still be filled with these reactions tumbling around in his head. Keeping him from sleep and even more keeping him from real, true thought. Thought that has the potential to change his life and the circumstances that he is in.

The noise of the world keeps out true thought and so one must take action against the numerous petty distractions to really reconnect with his thoughts. Setting aside an hour or so a day to be alone will do more to clear your mind than just about anything. Set aside an hour to read, to write, and to be alone. This will lead to your mind being emptied of worldly distractions. Turn off the TV, disconnect the internet, and stay away from the radio. This is time for you to be with you.

Reconnect With Yourself

    Many if not most people have forgotten who they are. They have forgotten what makes them, them. They fear being alone because they don't want to deal with the neglect they have given themselves. They don't want to deal with having to look themselves in the mirror and acknowledge where they are. But this is something that must be done. Problems don't get better by ignoring them they can only get worse.

When you spend time in quiet and solitude with yourself you reconnect with who you are. You reconnect with your true dreams, desires, and your true mission in life. Not the mission your parents, society, spouse, or anyone else put there but the one that you were born with. The one that connects with who you are on a fundamental level. The one that makes you feel alive and that fulfills you.

It can easily be forgotten when the voices of society and others are constantly being injected into our head. When you spend time with yourself alone it will take time to reconnect. If you were going to go see an old friend, you wouldn't spend ten minutes talking to him then leave. You would take your time because it is a relationship that you care deeply about and value. Well the relationship you have with yourself is even more important and valuable. It is the most important and valuable relationship that you have. Being true to yourself. It will take time for the thoughts and opinions of others to be cleared from your head and for your own thoughts and feelings to rise up. But you will notice them when they do. They are unmistakable. When you know who and what you are it gives you power during your day to day life. Because you operate with the confidence that you are operating how you want. You feel much more sure of yourself. When others doubt you or question you, you stay firm because you know what your true thoughts, opinions, and feelings are.

Focus on Life Goals

Reconnecting with yourself will inevitably lead to the resurfacing of your goals for your life. Which will allow you to focus on them. If you don't focus on something you can never hope to accomplish it. You've probably heard the saying "If you don't know where you're going any road will take you there". If you don't know your life goals your life will never end up where you want it to end up. Only once your goals are clear and true will you be able to make progress. Which you will get from focusing your mind and reconnecting with yourself. You must then focus on those goals until they are accomplished. You must keep them at the forefront of your mind so that they are not forgotten and drift back down to the deep recesses to be neglected.

    There are some things you should do to ensure that you are on your way to accomplishing your goals and achieving the life of your dreams. These things are powerful when done consistently.

    The first thing you must do is write down your goals every day. There is something about physically writing that activates your mind and helps to keep your goals at the forefront of your mind. For example is you listen to a speaker talk without writing notes then you listened to another speaker but wrote notes, which one would you remember better? Even without referring to the notes you would remember the one you took notes on better. Because you focused your mind by the writing process.

The second thing you must do is meditate on your goals. Meaning think about them often. Keep them in your mind. Think about them before you go to bed and think about them when you wake up in the morning. The more you think about them the more your mind will give you ideas and actions to take to accomplish them.

The third step is to visualize the accomplishment of your goals. Take five to ten minutes every day and visualize what it would look and feel like to have accomplished your goals. Visualization is very powerful for the mind. You can do this before bed as visualizing is a good way to focus your mind and wind down after a busy day or in the morning hours before the day has started.

The fourth and final step is to do all of these things consistently. Consistency is key. You do these things once, twice, for a week, or even a month and you won't see much result. You must do them day in and day out for a while. Having high goals is good, but these goals take time to accomplish.

Take time for solitude. To be alone with yourself and your thoughts. To get away from the hustle and bustle of the world and the stimulation of electronic devices and others. You will feel more at peace, more focused, and more connected with yourself when you do.

24 – Choose Your Life Or Have It Chosen For You

Every moment of every day your life is being decided. It is either being decided for you or being decided by you. Where you end up is a choice. Greatness, happiness, success, health, and wealth are available to all, yet so few actually get them. Why is this? The information is there. Yet how many people take a look at it? Or even if they do how many people actually dig into it instead of giving it a passing glance. How many people remember what they read and hear?

How many people get bogged down by stress and distractions? I think it's safe to say that the latter group is much larger than the former group.

What do you think the average age is that men give up on their dreams? Middle school? High school? College? Working their first "real" job? When is it, that we become miserable? Look at the majority of children they are happy and look at the majority of adults, they are miserable. At some point there is a disconnect. Children believe in themselves, adults do not. While I think the "be like children" thing can be overblown it does have valid points to it.

Is your life going in the direction that you want it to go? If you continue on the path you are on, will that get you where you want to go in a few years? Or does the path you are on never intersect with your goals and ideal life? If it doesn't you need to change your path now.

Your time is limited and every moment more of it is slipping away. Like the grains of an hour glass. They slowly but steadily drain out. Going back to having your life chosen for you, you'll notice that when we let others choose our life for us is when our spark usually dies.

When you were a child you disobeyed your parents at some point. Perhaps not intentionally or maliciously but you did something they didn't approve of at some point. We all do, it's human nature. You were likely corrected. This likely happened again and again. Then you were "corrected" by your teachers, other adults, and the media. Eventually you got it into your head that you couldn't trust yourself and your own judgement. You begin to rely on the opinion and ideals of others and of the masses. We are all put through this process. We ignore our own mind and heart. We end up living at odds with ourselves. When we live at odds with ourselves we run into all sorts of problems and no matter what happiness will elude us. Because we are living incongruently.

Look at it like this. Let's say you go up and talk to a pretty girl. You are attracted to her and want to have sex with her. Yet when you place your hand on her after a few moments you get nervous and take it off. She thinks that she's wasn't attractive enough and that you're not sure that you like her. So she begins to feel self-conscious. When she feels self-conscious you think it's because you touched her (and it was but in the opposite way of what you're thinking) and so now feel awkward and the interaction ends up going nowhere. You were not congruent. A congruent man would have kept his hand on the woman because he is attracted to her and so his actions would have lined up with his thoughts and heart.

When your mind (thoughts), body (actions), and heart (feelings) line up you are being congruent. There is a lot of power in being congruent. You will walk through this earth unique and everyone will have a powerful reaction to you. They will either love you because you are expressing your true self or they will hate you because they know that they themselves are not expressing their true selves. It's like poor people who hate the rich, people who don't get laid who hate guys who do, Feminists who hate housewives because they have families and a man who is attracted to them. Essentially envy. You can't let the envy of others effect you. It's not your problem. Live your life in the way that is most beneficial to you and let others deal with their own issues. Doesn't mean you can't offer help just don't get bogged down by others. Most miserable people don't want help they want to drag others down with them so they can validate their world view, don't get sucked in.

How you spend your time is how your life ends up. We've talked about the importance of goal setting and how to set them. We talked about mediating on them and visualizing them. Something else that is very important to success is writing down the most important things you can do every day. The night before I write down six things that are the most important for the next day. So the list might include writing a chapter in my current book, networking for my business, writing a post for my site, and so on and so forth. Every day no matter what I make sure that I accomplish these six things. Of course like everything else this must be done with consistency if it is going to have any positive effect. Doing it once or twice is not going to get you anywhere.

    Keep in mind that every moment you are choosing your life. Even when sitting back and watching TV you are choosing your life. When you listen to the opinions of the masses over your own heart you are letting others choose your life for you. This will never lead to being fulfilled because of the simple fact that others are not you. Most men never realize their life is a result of their choices. They blame others, society, and fate. When those things can only have control of your life if you let them. They cannot do anything without your permission. You either choose your life or it is chosen for you, decide wisely.

25 – Sanity Is Assumed

We live in a world where sanity is assumed for the majority of the populace. After all if the majority is doing it then it must be right. You know democracy and all that. Unfortunately this isn't quite the reality. We like to assume that those around us know what they are doing. That the majority of people around us have an idea of what's going on. Sure, maybe the crackheads, bums, and other degenerates are lost but the majority of people? No way society wouldn't function if everyone didn't know what they were doing.

I'll have to disagree with that. If the majority of people knew what they were doing, if the majority of people had a clue society would be much different. However sanity is assumed because there would be a panic otherwise. People would have to question their lives and actually might have to change and learn.

The point I'm getting at here is that you should question what you are told. You should investigate and find out the truth behind things. Do not blindly accept whatever the dominant narrative is. There is so much spin, misdirection, and blatant lies that fill up what we hear and see. It takes a perceptive mind to cut through all the B.S. that is out there.

What we hear on the TV, radio, and books is all designed with a specific purpose in mind. And that purpose is not to educate you. That purpose is to get you to act and think in a certain way for a certain reason. This includes the majority of "alternative" currents out there as well. The masses of people do not think original thoughts, they think the thoughts that were put there.

Thousands of years ago populaces were controlled through religious systems. Many empires even made the king or emperor the

God of the empire's religion. They controlled the populace through an intricate religious system dominated by high priests. These priests would make dictates to the populace and say that they were from the gods. The people, being lowly mortals, would have no choice but to blindly accept the dictates. After all they were from the gods. So what would a mere man be to question the gods? This didn't stop some truly inquisitive and brave minds but it was enough to keep the populace in check.

    Remember the manifestation of principles change, but the principles themselves do not. We have the same system going on in our modern "enlightened" world. While the idea of "gods" and religion itself is mocked and ridiculed in our modern world, we still blindly follow dictates. People are still controlled and led like sheep to the slaughter. The new religion goes under different names "progressivism", "social justice", "one or new world order" and so on and so forth. There are sins such as questioning the narrative, thinking certain thoughts deemed "hateful, bigoted, or some ism/phobic" by the controllers, and thinking on your own. We still have witch hunts and soon will most likely have burnings at the stake of our own. Humanity has not changed and it never will. People nowadays like to pretend they are brave by "standing up" against religion or other bugaboos of the past. Ideals and cultures that are defeated and denigrated. These people are about as brave as someone kicking a crippled man lying on the ground.

    True kings do not go along with the tide. They understand the mechanisms of populace control. They understand how the matrix works. They understand that there is more going on than meets the eye. They're not fools though those they lead may be. When everyone around them thinks the same thoughts, acts the same way, and believes the same thing. The king stands his ground and goes his own way. The king understands why the people act the way in which they do. He tries to help those he can but otherwise focuses on his own path. Remember most people will fight against what is good for them and they are not worth your time. Only those who have a desire to learn, to improve, to change are worth your time.

You may have heard of conspiracy theories regarding how the world functions. An elite council who dictates the wars, economic policies, and political policy of the world. While there are bad eggs in the conspiracy theory genre there is much truth. I'm not saying to go and devour every conspiracy theory book fully and without question. You should never devour anything without question. What I'm saying is that there is much wisdom in those books. There are connections that the average people miss. When I read books like these while much of it I discard there are always a few ideas that ring true. While maybe the author's exact description didn't ring true the idea behind it did. You then begin to notice patterns in the way that society functions. You see that things are not as random as they appear. But that they have a rhyme and reason behind them.

Look for patterns, be aware of the way in which the world works. Stay away from the mainstream news and ways of thinking. Don't get caught up in the fads of the masses. The scandals, the events, the bullshit. Take a step back and see what is truly happening. Don't let yourself get caught up in it, but understand why others do.

Stand apart from the crowd. Understand how the puppet masters think and you will avoid getting caught up in all the traps that they have set. You will be able to be free and truly free because you have freed yourself from the lies. Like it says in the Bible "Then you shall know the truth, and the truth shall set you free". You cannot build a solid foundation for your life, manhood, and kingship upon lies or foolishness. It must be built upon the rock solid foundation of truth and wisdom. Live in the world but don't be of the world.

26 – Life Is A Choice

One of the main thrusts of this book is that your entire life is a decision, a choice. That you decide where it is you end up. Living the life of your dreams or broke in a gutter. It is up to you. What you do moment by moment is what makes your overall life.

Your brain is the most powerful tool that is known to man and it was given freely. So most do not appreciate it. With your mind operating on your brain you have the power to accomplish anything. Ultimately it is your mindset that matters. It is your mindset that will make or break you. Riches, friends, family, women, all can come and go. But your mind is you and therefore it will always be with you. You must utilize it and have it work for you. The body is servant to the mind. Your life is servant to your mind.

Whatever your mindset is, is where your life will end up. So if you day in and day out always talk about how fate is against you, that you are a victim of circumstances, and other whining thoughts you will end up with a bad life because you are thinking bad thoughts which will lead to bad action or no action (which is in a way bad action). I've used illustrations throughout this book of men who took different paths in life. They had different starting points and different makeups yet none of that ended up mattering in the long run. Sure, starting out ahead is nice. And if you have started out with a leg up then by all means take it and don't feel bad about it. Remember where a person ends up is their own fault. Let me say that again. Where a person ends up is their own fault. What a person's life is, is their own fault. Don't pity people offer them the way and if they reject it then move on. They are not your problem. They most likely just want you to be miserable like them.

That's what their life has become. Making as many people as possible miserable to validate their own world view. They live small lives and when they see others who don't they know that it is their own fault for where they are. These people are poison and cancerous. Don't feel pity for them or engage with them. Ignore them, live your own life. Don't get caught up in their tide of negativity it will only drag you down. Don't let them guilt or manipulate you. Avoid them completely.

 Many people spin their wheels for years without going anywhere. The get stuck in ruts and never get out. Some keep spinning furiously, like a hamster in his wheel, hoping that they will get out. While others give up after so long, saying that it's hopeless. These people do not have the right mindset. Working furiously while it can be good at certain points and at certain times will not get you where you want to go in and of itself. Hard work is important but it is not the whole story. While you should do both if you had to choose between a proper mindset and working hard the proper mindset would get you farther.

    It is the single largest determining factor of your life. Nothing comes close. You've probably seen complete idiots that have their own businesses and are making millions, you've seen out of shape losers with smoking hot girls, you've seen men who are happy living in a shack in a war torn country. It is mindset. Mindset is what enabled these individuals to do the seemingly impossible. Their mindset is different from others, their mindset works for them instead of against them. It opens up a world of opportunities that they are more than happy to take.

The world is a place of abundance, remember that. No matter what you couldn't make all the money, sleep with all the beautiful women, or take all the happiness. The last one seemed obvious but the others are just as true. Change your mindset to reflect this truth. Every day you are hammered with talk of scarcity and the hardness of life yet there are people who live lives filled with abundance and ease. While there will certainly be hard time in life and you must meet the challenges of life many people make things harder than they should because in their mind things being hard equals you're doing it right. Though this can be the case in things like working out, disciplining yourself to a schedule, and producing great works it doesn't apply to everything.

Don't make easy things hard and think that your life will be better because of it. Hardness in and of itself is not what causes you to mature, learn, and grow. Yet some people think this and then proceed to make their lives as hard as possible. Don't do this, don't work against yourself. Things that are hard will naturally be hard, you don't have to help it along.

    Some things will be hard and others easy. Don't make things hard on purpose. Remember your life is a choice. So make the decisions that will make your life better and the lives of those who are around you better. Develop yourself and others will benefit from it. Focus on yourself and others will be affected by it in a positive way. Become a great king and the subjects will naturally benefit. Make no mistake someone will take the kingship. Someone always rises. There is always a king, there is always a leader. If it's not you than it will be someone else. Claim your rightful place as king of your life and king of your mind.

Don't let others usurp your throne and run the kingdom recklessly. As so many do. If you are not in control of your mind then you are not in control of your destiny. Then you won't end up where it is that you want to end up. Others cannot lead you where you want to go, they cannot lead you to your ultimate destiny. Others can certainly help (although they more often hinder) you on your path but only you can walk it and walk it you must.

27 – Guilt

Of all the emotions few have the potential to sabotage your progress like guilt. While there are certainly times to feel guilty. As in when you have violated your own principles. Most of the time guilt is used as a weapon by the weak to destroy the strong and bring them down to their level.

When you are making it in this world you shouldn't feel guilty. You'll often see that successful people freely show others the way yet are ignored. The secrets of success are not secrets they are things that have been said by millions of people millions of times.

They are not hard to find for those who are looking. Seek and you shall find. However most people do not seek let alone ask or knock and therefore will never find what they are looking for. Then when they see others get ahead of them they get envious and jealous. They begin plotting against them and resenting them. There are entire political parties and movements built around the resentment of the success of others. Very popular ones too.

    You see this with healthy young men who upon entering puberty (as children often ignore adults, often to their benefit) their entire mindset changed. They are made to feel guilty for being male, a certain race, rich, successful, good with girls, or whatever. For being who it is that they are. They are made to feel guilty because of envy and jealously. The shaming and guilt is applied until the boy accepts being a loser. Then the attacks will stop because the crab has successfully been pulled back into the bucket. They never understand that if they kept going they would have made it out of the bucket entirely. This continues until their death.

    You cannot let others make you feel guilty for being who you are, or for anything for that matter. Guilt is a control mechanism, nothing less and nothing more. When it is a control mechanism you enforce on yourself it is good. For example say in high school a friend tells you a couple of kids said they are going to jump him so you tell him you'll have his back. Then you get caught up in something and your friend gets beat up. You will feel guilty and you should feel guilty. Because you violated your own principles. You should have been there for your friend and had his back.

    Guilt can also be used as a negative control mechanism. Say that a lot of girls like you and other men see this. Jealous men projecting their own insecurities on you will call you everything from "asshole" to "douchebag" to "misogynist" and more.

When you are proud of yourself others will shame you until you bow back down. When you have an unpopular political stance people will shame or even physically assault you (another reason why it pays to learn self-defense so you can put people in their place) to get you to not have that particular view. The use of shame and guilt runs deep in our society. Like stated before we still have a control "religion" of sorts, it has just changed names.

Kings are not affected by guilt or shame, unless it comes from within. Kings could care less what the unwashed masses, the plebian hordes, the crabs in the bucket think. Why would they? Who cares what the miserable, what the losers think. This isn't to say that everyone who isn't rich or successful is a loser. No, not at all. There are plenty of great people who are part of the masses. What it is saying is that you shouldn't care what the masses think, you are the king. Wouldn't it be weird and unnatural if God took the advice of man when it went against his own? Of course it would. This doesn't mean that God hates man of course simply that he knows best. He is above man yet still cares about man. The king should do the same. He should be above the common while not hating the common but helping those who are worthy of his help.

Keep your mind like a well-guarded fortress. Remember the analogy of your conscious mind working as a gatekeeper? Be a dutiful gatekeeper. Ruthlessly keep out and exterminate anything that could threaten the wellness and health of your mind. Of your inner sanctum. Nothing and no one is worth your life. Nothing is worth giving up your own well-being. Don't let others manipulate you into things. Stand firm and strong in your own beliefs. Do not bow before the tests of others. While they may not like you, they may even hate you for your views, the fact that you stand your ground will make the world respect you. If you have a choice between being liked and being respected, take being respected every time.

Guilt has stopped more men from greatness than just about anything else. It has caused more people to limit themselves than anything else. It has caused countless failures and countless unfulfilled lives. It can be just, if not more, destructive than anger, hatred, jealously, or any other negative emotion. Beware guilt. Unlike the others guilt innately plays on your sense of goodness using it against you. Guilt when used in this way a truly sick and disgusting trick. Do not feel guilty because of what other people say, think, or do. The only reason on this earth that you should ever feel guilty is because you have violated your own personal standard. That is it.

    Learn the difference between healthy guilt and unhealthy guilt. Guilt you feel when you have violate your own principles is healthy guilt. Guilt foisted on you by others is unhealthy guilt. When people learn that you cannot be changed with shame and guilt they lose their power over you. That is the power of the lower over the higher the power of guilt. That is what keeps the superior higher from crushing the inferior lower even when the inferior lower deserves it. A good king crushes those who need to be crushed and helps those who need to be helped. Be a good king.

28 – The Purpose of Kingship

Some of you may ask what is the point of being a king? What is the goal of a king? What is a king's life purpose? While there will be some difference between people there are things that are similar to all. These goals will manifest themselves in different ways but the principles remain the same. The purpose of kingship is to help others, guide others, to be a leader and light the way for those who will follow you. To make the things that were hard for you easy for others. To improve the world through your work and influence.

When most people talk about improving the world they do it through nice sounding but ultimately empty platitudes. They think that by working at a soup kitchen or that by giving to the needy that they are improving the world. While there is obviously nothing wrong with doing those things is it really changing the world? Sure it helps but it is the best way to go about changing the world? For example you may not like this but Henry Ford has done far more to help the world than Mother Teresa ever did. His inventions and ideas revolutionized the world making countless lives better. I'm not saying this to denigrate Mother Teresa only to prove a point. What most people think of when they think of improving the world really doesn't do that much.

Filling a person's need helps them. Teaching someone how to do something helps them. Carnegie by building libraries across the United States has done more to combat poverty than welfare ever did. Of course most of those in poverty do not avail themselves of the resources around them hence they stay in poverty. While giving someone a meal or a dime may make you feel good, there are much more effective ways of changing the world.

So when I say improve the world, I mean actually improve it. Like Telsa, Ford, and others have done. Improving the world is something concrete and realistic not mindless hippy platitudes.

Make Easy for Others, What Was Hard for You

The phrase above just about sums up the purpose of business. That and to fill a need. When you are successful and truly successful you will want to give back to others. You will want to make the world a better place. You will want others to live the life of their dreams because you yourself are living the life of your dreams. You know that it is possible. You know that it requires a certain mindset, hard work, and time.

 A good example of this is an entrepreneur named MJ DeMarco he wrote the book *The Millionaire Fastlane* which I highly recommend you pick up. Anyways before writing the book MJ had already made his money through selling his website and a couple other means. He did not write the book to make money in and of itself. While I do not remember the exact story MJ wanted to give others the blue print for getting to the place that he got in life. He wanted others to be able to achieve success and riches. So MJ studied and went through the success and failures of his own life until he came up with *The Millionaire Fastlane*. While it took MJ years and years to learn everything that is contained in *The Millionaire Fastlane* the book can be read in a week, or even a day if you really wanted. The knowledge that was hard for MJ to acquire he has made easy for you to acquire.

MJ took what was hard for him and made it easy for others. This is essentially what good books, coaching, and programs are. Making easy for you what was hard for them. For example it has taken me years to understand the principles contained in this book. I remember in high school hearing one of my teachers talk about mindset but didn't pay attention. It took me tons of failing before realizing what works and what doesn't. Of course I have been helped by others along the way as well. I can't remember the exact reason why I started reading books but I soon became addicted because of how much they accelerated my learning, growth, and life. I didn't have to continuously blunder ahead in the dark. Books serve to help illuminate the path that you want to go down. They help you avoid detours, traps, and ruts. The reason books do this is because they contain knowledge.

Imagine this. You are standing on a rocky outcrop high on some mountain. There is a very low level of light you can barely see a few feet in front of you. You know that the direction you want to go in is ahead of you. Between you and your destination there are tons of drop offs that could cripple you, jagged rocks that could cut or hamstring you, and impassable walls you could spend eternity trying to get over. Knowledge serves as a light. The more knowledge that you acquire the brighter your light grows. So some may walk their path with light beaming out of them. They see the majority of obstacles a mile away. While others move about blind. They stumble and crash hoping that by generating enough movement that they will end up where they want, a strategy that rarely if ever works. There are opportunities to gain knowledge, to increase your light all around you. But we must take them, otherwise we will end up like the blind stumbling forward hoping and wishing for the best that will never come.

Give Back

You will never feel truly fulfilled unless you are giving back to the world. You can do this in a variety of ways. Money though the most popular in only one of them. You can give your time as well but the most valuable thing that you can give others is your knowledge. Give a man your riches and if he loses them he is lost but give a man the knowledge of how you acquired your riches and he will never be lost. Like the old saying goes. Give a man a fish and you feed him for a day, teach a man to fish and you feed him for a lifetime. Save your time for your loved ones and those who you enjoy being around, save your money for charities or research that would benefit from it, give back your knowledge to the masses.

It is your knowledge that has the potential to do the most good for them. It is your knowledge that has the potential to change their lives for the better. It is your knowledge that has the potential to help them achieve their dreams. When you have achieved success you will want to give back and this is the best way to do it. If you have knowledge do not keep it to yourself, if it is valuable share it with others. Write books, start a website, shoot video do whatever it is you must. If you have light share it with others don't keep it to yourself. In doing so you will be more fulfilled while helping others and you will be fulfilling your purpose as a king.

29 – 10 Steps to Begin Your Ascent

Alright so the majority of this book has been big picture stuff. Now I want to give you some immediately actionable advice to get you started on the path to claiming your kingship and cultivating the right mindset. Reading this book was a great start but all learning must continue. You must constantly grow every day.

Step 1 – Read Everyday

Knowledge is power. When I say read every day I mean books. Not blogs, articles, or magazines.

While all of those things have value they are not the same as reading a book. Every day your mind should grow. You should be exposed to new ideas or see another view of an old idea.

    I've heard it said that knowledge isn't power only applied knowledge is. I think this is obvious. That would be like saying guns won't protect you they only protect you if you load them and pull the trigger. No kidding right? Anyways when you acquire knowledge if it helps you then you will naturally want to apply it. Don't concern yourself with acting on every single last thing you read. I see people get obsessively caught up in this. By reading it, it becomes a part of you. Then when you take action you can't help but be affected by what you have read and learned. Look at the big picture don't get caught up in every minute detail.

Step 2 – Affirmations

Some people are uncomfortable with the idea of affirmations. They think that others will judge them for it or that if they need affirmations then something is wrong with them. While the first one you can't do anything about and shouldn't care about the second one is completely false. Your mind is programmed by what it is constantly exposed to. You become what you think about.

No one and I mean no one is naturally born with a perfect mindset. Even with the ideal childhood and a wonderful upbringing everyone can be doing better in this regard. My suggestion would be to take ten affirmations. That is things you want to be and say them to yourself in the mirror three times each and every morning and every night. Look yourself in the eye when you do these and try to convey as much feeling as possible. You may feel self-conscious and uncomfortable at first. This is fine push through the uncomfortable feelings and they will disappear.

Step 3 – Write Out Goals Everyday

You should be writing out your goals every day. Not just thinking about them (though you should be doing that as well) but physically writing them out. I would suggest that you use pen and paper instead of a word processor as well. There is a unique power in physical writing something out. Your mind has a much easier time of focusing on it and remembering it when it is physically written.

We all have different goals for different parts of our lives. I write down my top ten every morning and every night. I don't necessarily write them out word for word as exact copies each and every time but try to write them from memory. I find that this also helps me to remember and focus on them when I have to remember them the next morning or later that night.

Step 4 – Watch Good Videos

    YouTube is a great resource. While it can be used as a great time waster it can also be used as your own personal university on whatever it is you want to learn about. I personally try to do a write up of a YouTube video every day.

I keep a playlist of videos that I find interesting and try to watch at least one a day. Even if they are short twelve minute videos if they are educational they are good. We all learn in different ways. Some are more visual learners while others are more kinesthetic and so on and so forth. While I think this idea has been blown out of proportion and limits people because they shut off to certain forms of knowledge because "it's not their style" there are many benefits to receiving knowledge in different ways. You would have to pay big bucks to go to lectures that might not even be worth it. YouTube allows you to watch lectures and talks for free and if they suck you can leave them right away. Take advantage of this resource and try to watch at least one educational video a day.

Step 5 – Write Down A Plan

Like stated before there is a certain definite power in the written word. When you make physical manifestations of your thoughts through the written word it helps your mind to focus and remember. Having goals is great but it also helps to have a written plan for your life. You can do this on a monthly or weekly basis, personally I prefer taking one day each month to really dig down and write things out.

This plan is the plan for your life. Where you want to see improvements and how you are going to get to those improvements. Let's use you want to bring more traffic to your blog as an example. You would sit down and write the goal "More traffic to blog" at the top of the page. Then you would write ten ways in which a blog can generate traffic. Then you write down two or three ways in which you could utilize each method. So say you have writing guest posts as your first way to generate traffic. You would then go and write down three blogs that you could write a guest post for and what that guest post would be. These are not set in stone but are designed to get your mind thinking about it. You would then proceed to do this for each of your goals. You can see how doing this weekly could be a bit much, but if you find it works for you then by all means do it.

Step 6 – Become An Expert

Each of us makes our living in some way. Take a step every day to be the best at your job. If you are in sales read sales books, listen to sales lectures, take sales training, practice sales with others, do something each and every day that is going to put you ahead of the pack.

Whatever field you are in become an expert in that field. Learn all that you can about the subject. Listen to all the experts see where they agree and disagree and then come to your own conclusions. Constantly bring in new knowledge, learning, and ideas into your mind. You will rise above all the others in your field.

Step 7 – Share

Share what you have learned with others. Like I've said before make easy for others what was hard for you. Sure some won't listen but you shouldn't concern yourself with them. Don't preach or moralize, but share. Share because you truly want to benefit and help others. If you see a problem and know the solution to it, it would be cruel to keep it from that person.

It's crazy how many people go around knowing the answer to each other's problems yet say nothing. I'm not talking about strangers, I mean close friends as well. We've all heard and thought "well why didn't you say something?". Don't hold back the truth, don't hold back what is good. Sometimes it may hurt, sometimes it may sting, but it is ultimately healing.

Step 9 – Enjoy Life And Have Fun

Improving yourself, building your empire, claiming your kingship are all worthy goals that take commitment, hard work, and right knowledge to be accomplished. However you should never forget to have fun. To let loose and enjoy life. Life isn't meant to be one long grind to the grave. Those who get the most out of life always have good times and know that fun is an essential part of life.

Take time to go out and do things that you want to do. Different people have different ideas of fun. For one person it might be visiting the historic sites in Europe for another it might be going to Vegas. Or both. You know what you want to do, take time to do it. Don't put off having fun and enjoying life.

Step 10 – Visualize Everyday

Visualizing is one of the most powerful tools to achieving the life that you want. I'll be honest I was very skeptical of visualization for the longest time. I am a very practical man and it seemed a bit esoteric. However I was wrong. Visualization is an essential part of how your mind works and getting it to go in the direction of your goals and dreams.

Here is my particular visualization session you can modify it as you see fit. First off I don't do this when I know I will be distracted or interrupted. Sometimes it is early in the morning other times it is late at night. Take time whenever you get a chance. I usually put in headphones and listen to a meditation track that lasts about ten to fifteen minutes. I listen to different tracks but have a few favorites that I usually rotate between. I lie down and relax clearing my mind. I then start the track and visualize the completion of my goals. I pick the ten that I wrote down. I don't have a set time limit for each one but always have time to get through each of them. I visualize what it would be like to accomplish them. What it would feel like. The ways to get there and the actual act of getting there. I do this every day.

Wrap-up

Hopefully these tips have given you some things to think about and some practices to start getting the right mindset. Perhaps you already do some of these, perhaps you already do all of these. Good then you are well on your way to becoming a king. Remember for these things to be effective they must be done continuously and consistently. I don't know how many people I've heard who have visualized for a week then come back and say "Hey I visualized making millions and it hasn't happened yet visualization doesn't work". It isn't magic, it's a practice for your mind. It is about getting your mind right.

If you think things will just happen and fall in place you're in for a long line of disappointments, that's not the way it works. Remember it's not magic, it's practice. Like working out isn't magic. Can you imagine someone saying "Hey man so I curled like ten times this week and my arms haven't even grown an inch working out is bullshit". It's the same for these mind practices. They take consistent effort. It's harder to see progress because the progress isn't something you can just look in the mirror and see. But it is there and it is happening. Like the wind you can't see it but you know when it's there.

30 – 21 Attributes of A King

We've covered many attributes of a king in this book. Attributes that you have already begun to embody or at the very least are becoming aware of them through this book. This chapter will serve as a summary or reminder of what we have covered. Refer to it when you want a fresh reminder of the attributes that you want to embody and live out in your day to day life.

1 – Irrational Self-Confidence

A king believes in himself and who he is one hundred percent. It doesn't matter what others think. It doesn't matter what might appear "rational". A king has an unwavering belief in himself. He never doubts himself. If every single individual in the world said a king couldn't do something and he wanted to do it, he would still do it.

2 – Growth Mindset

Kings know that growth is eternal. They know that they must grow every day for the rest of their lives and perhaps even further. They are constantly learning, testing, and refining themselves. They know to reach new heights they must grow into those new heights. They know that stagnation equals death.

3 – Self-Determined

A king goes his own way and does his own thing. While he will listen to the wise and respect those that deserve to be respected ultimately he is his own man who goes his own way. He doesn't need others to propel him to action, he knows where he wants to go and takes actions to reach that destination every day. He doesn't need others, he is his own motivation and direction.

4 – Risk Taker

A king knows that taking risks are an essential part of life. That risks are not bad or something to be avoided. Risks are essential and healthy. He takes risks and doesn't mind putting himself on the line. He knows that you can only win on offense. He has overridden the conditioning from when he was young when he was always told to be careful and put safety first. Now be puts life and growth first because he is no longer a boy but a king and a man.

5 – Focuses On Being Great Not Good

Kings know that being good is a trap. They know that when you have achieved the level of good or you become good at something that there is a chance that you will stay there. Kings know that comfort can be a deadly enemy. Kings push past being good into the realm of being great. They do not let the comfort of being good make them lazy or complacent they know that kings are great not good. Kings are the highest in the land not mid-tier.

6 – Doesn't Fear Failing

Kings know that failing is a part of success. They know that you fail towards success. They don't seek out failure for the sake of failing but they do not fear failure when it comes either. They see failure as a learning opportunity to grow and better themselves. They know that the fear of failure will keep you trapped and prevent you from achieving success.

7 – Is A Trigger Puller

Kings take action when the time comes to take action. They don't hang around and mull things over. They pull the trigger. They don't make excuses or think "maybe another time would be better". They take action. They know it's better to err on the side of taking action than on the side of hesitation. They know without action nothing gets done.

8 – Goes Against The Grain

Kings are above the masses. They have no problem going against the will of the masses or going against what they are told to do. They go their own way and stick to their path. They are not brought down by the constraints and chain that society, family, or friends may try to place on them. Kings go against the grain because they know the truth about the masses and live life as lions not sheep.

9 – Takes Charge

Kings assume the leadership role. They take charge of whatever circumstance or position that they are in. They naturally feel that the head role is their own so they take it naturally. They don't wait for others to take them where they want to go, kings take the lead and go themselves. And if others want to join them great, and if not also great. A king is on his own path and he is always leading the way.

10 – Has The Right Mindset

Kings know without the right mindset nothing can be accomplished. Even with every advantage given to an individual if they do not have the right mindset they will end up lost and lose to an individual who has the right mindset. Mindset is the ultimate advantage. Kings know that if you have it then you can do anything and that if you do not have it then you can do nothing. Kings understand the extreme importance of having the right mindset.

11 – Works Hard

Kings know that the lazy do not succeed. That those who try to take shortcuts end up losing. They know that to get where they want they will have to put in the work day in and day out. Kings do not shy away from hard work but rather embrace it because they know that goals worth having and worth achieving are not done without hard work.

12 – Works Smart

Kings know that in addition to working hard they must work smart. Some of the poorest peasants are the hardest workers but they will never get anywhere because they are not working smart in addition to working hard. Likewise some with limitless talent will get nowhere because they refuse to work hard but are always trying to skimp by on the least amount of effort possible. Kings avoid both of these extremes and know that both are needed. You must work hard and work smart, neither one is optional.

13 – Never Compromises

Kings know that compromise is not a virtue but an evil. Kings follow the truth and will not compromise it with lies. Kings remain firm in their convictions. They do not waver.

They are like a mountain. Come storms, man, or anything else and they stand firm. Kings do not change for others, especially not for the masses or society. A king does not compromise himself or his beliefs.

14 – Is Positive

A king knows that negativity and pessimism are the marks of small weak minds. A king has an optimistic view of life and knows that things are good. He isn't blind and Pollyanna in his outlook. He is realistic but also positive. This is not the feel good "fake a smile" type "happiness" that comes from an empty mind this is the optimism that comes from a strong mind. A king has a positive mental outlook on life.

15 – Is Self-Educated

A king knows that the only true education is self-education. There are kings who dropped out of grade school and paupers who have their doctorates. Kings know that formal education while occasionally helpful is not real education in any way, shape, or form. A king takes it upon himself to learn about his world and his subject of expertise. He takes matters into his own hands. He reads book, listens to lectures, and gains knowledge through his own means. He knows that good library is infinitely more valuable than a degree from the most prestigious college or institute.

16 – Gets Rid Of Any Limiting Beliefs

A king knows that his mind is the deciding factor in his life. He knows that if he has any limiting beliefs they will stop him from achieving what he could really achieve. A king never says he can't do something. He takes action and continues to take action until he either does it or decides there are better uses of his time. He never says that something is impossible or that he can't do it. He gets rid of any and all limiting beliefs. If he is to be limited it will be by physics and reality not himself.

17 – Takes Time To Be Alone

A king knows that he must spend time away from the maddening crowd. He must take time to separate himself from women, society, and even close friends and be with himself. He may do this by going out in nature or having a study where he can lose himself in meditation and deep thought. But regardless of how he does it, he does do it. Time alone is some of the most valuable time that a man can spend. To get away from the noise and discord of the society.

Solitude is paramount to being a good king.

18 – Doesn't Let Others Guilt Him

A king is not controlled by guilt or shame. He does not let others control him. He refuses to bow down to the shaming and guilt tactics of others. Others do not have control over the king, the king has control over himself. He is not swayed by the crowd or by society. He is not manipulated. He realizes that guilt and shame are tools used by the weak to control the strong and will take not part in being controlled by others. He stands his ground and never backs down from his beliefs, thoughts, and opinions.

He is too wise to be controlled by guilt or shame.

19 – Is A Leader

A king lights the way. He is the general leading from the front. The one the warriors love and respect. A king sets an example for others to follow. He shows the way for those who come after him. He is a leader. When others think of him they see him as someone to look up to, to emulate. Not because society or the crowd said to but because they came to that conclusion on their own. The king acts in the way that he does and sets an example for all to follow. A king leads and is a leader.

20 – Has A Purpose

A king has a deep purpose. A lifelong goal, a dream that he works day and night to bring forth into existence. A king knows his life purpose. He knows the path that he wants to travel. He has put time, thought, and effort into its achievement. He lives with an accurate compass pointing him in the direction that he needs to go. He is not tossed back and forth by the ebb and flow of the world. He has a guiding light that always keeps him on his path. A north star of his dream. He keeps his focus on it and nears it every day. When he does reach it he knows that there will be another beyond it and so on and so forth. A king always has a purpose and direction for his life.

21 – Gives Back

A king gives back to the world. He gives his time to the ones he loves and enjoys spending time with. He gives his money to charities or research that he thinks will help the world in true ways. He gives his knowledge to the masses so that they may improve their lives and one day join him in kingship. He knows that improving the lives of others is a worthwhile task and that without giving back it will hard for him to ultimately be fulfilled. Often the ones who are most generous are those who we would least expect.

They do not make big fanfares of the event they simply do it because it is what they want to do. They want to make easy for others what was hard for them. Nothing more and nothing less.

Kingship is a journey. It is a journey to get there and then a journey once you have acquired it. By embodying the principles discussed in this book and referring to this list you will be well on your way to becoming a king and living the life of your dreams. There will be hard times and times when it seems like no progress is being made. But you must continue to work at it. Like they say "Rome wasn't built in a day". No kingdom is. By consistent work you will acquire it. Have faith and stay strong. I hope to see you all as kings one day.

About the Author

Enjoyed the content? Then could you do me a favor? Leave a review on Amazon or tell a friend about the ways that the book has helped you. I love reading how my books have positively affected the lives of my readers. I read each and every review, they mean a lot to me. If you want to learn more I run a blog at charlessledge.com where you can find more content to further your masculine development to new heights. If you found value in the book drop by and join the community. Looking forward to hearing from you.

                      -Charles Sledge